PENGUIN BOOKS

TEST YOUR IQ

Professor Hans J. Eysenck was born in 1916 and received a Ph.D. in psychology from London University. He is a Professor Emeritus from the University of London. A frequent lecturer, he has been a visiting professor at the University of Pennsylvania and the University of California. Though known mostly for his experimental research in the field of personality, which yielded some eight hundred articles, Professor Eysenck is the author of numerous books, including *Know Your Own IQ* and *Check Your Own IQ*.

Test Your IQ

Hans Eysenck with Darrin Evans

PENGUIN BOOKS

PENGUIN BOOKS

Published by the Penguin Group

Penguin Group (USA) Inc., 375 Hudson Street, New York, New York 10014, U.S.A.

Penguin Group (Canada), 10 Alcorn Avenue, Toronto,

Ontario, Canada M4V 3B2 (a division of Pearson Penguin Canada Inc.)

Penguin Books Ltd, 80 Strand, London WC2R 0RL, England

Penguin Ireland, 25 St Stephen's Green, Dublin 2, Ireland (a division of Penguin Books Ltd)

Penguin Group (Australia), 250 Camberwell Road, Camberwell,

Victoria 3124, Australia (a division of Pearson Australia Group Pty Ltd)

Penguin Books India Pvt Ltd, 11 Community Centre,

Panchsheel Park, New Delhi – 110 017, India

Penguin Group (NZ), cnr Airborne and Rosedale Roads,

Albany, Auckland, New Zealand (a division of Pearson New Zealand Ltd)

Penguin Books (South Africa) (Pty) Ltd, 24 Sturdee Avenue,

Rosebank, Johannesburg 2196, South Africa

Penguin Books Ltd, Registered Offices: 80 Strand, London WC2R 0RL, England

First published in Great Britian by Thorsons 1994
First published in the United States of America
in Penguin Books 1995

13 15 17 19 20 18 16 14

Copyright © Hans Eysenck and Darrin Evans, 1994
All rights reserved

The publishers would like to thank the following people for their
assistance: P. Boocock, David Chenery, B. Clarke, Anne Clinch,
K. Evans, Pia Genge, G. L. Gymer, Stephen Hatfield, Jo Jackson,
Lisa Miles, Roslyn Sharp, Dean Turney

ISBN 0 14 02.4962 1
(CIP data available)

Printed in the United States of America
Set in Cheltenham Book

Except in the United States of America, this book is sold subject to
the condition that it shall not, by way of trade or otherwise, be lent,
re-sold, hired out, or otherwise circulated without the publisher's
prior consent in any form of binding or cover other than that in
which it is published and without a similar condition including this
condition being imposed on the subsequent purchaser.

Contents

PART ONE

PART TWO

PART THREE

Test Your IQ

Part One:

The Meaning and Measurement of IQ

The notion of the IQ (intelligence quotient) is perhaps the only technical term in modern psychology that has really achieved popularity, and IQ testing is perhaps the only aspect of applied psychology that is at all widely used. Yet most people will have received contrasting messages about the IQ. On the one hand it is praised highly as one of the great achievements of modern psychology, the first mental quality to be measured along scientific lines, and the first measurement to have proved its usefulness. On the other hand there are numerous detractors saying that all the IQ does is to tell you how well you can do IQ tests; that psychologists have no idea of what intelligence is, and cannot even agree on a proper definition; and that its practical, application as for instance in school selection procedures, has been a disaster. Who is right?

When you look a little closer, you will find one astonishing thing. Those who criticise the IQ along these lines are all laypeople without any proper training in the relevant specialities of modern psychology – child development, educational psychology, behavioural genetics, and psychometrics (the design and use of psychological tests). Furthermore, they have no experience in constructing, using and experimenting with IQ tests. In Snyderman and Rothman's book *The IQ Controversy* (Oxford, Transaction Books, 1988) the authors questioned over 600 experts in all the fields mentioned above; they found considerable agreement, often virtual unanimity, on all points. Consider the most important question: what do IQ tests measure? Of the experts, 99.3 per cent agreed that it measured the ability to think abstractly, to reason; 97.7 per cent that it measured problem-solving ability; 96 per cent that it measured the capacity to acquire knowledge. That is a good level of agreement; failure to achieve 100-per-cent agreement is due to individual preferences for one of these more-or-less equivalent descriptions over the other. Thus, experts do *not* disagree about what IQ tests measure; they show widespread agreement.

Why do the critics deny this? Snyderman and Rothman argued that disagreement comes from journalists, book reviewers, television personalities and others in the media who have no expert knowledge in this field, but whose political views and attitudes are hostile to the very notion of scientific measurement of psychological variables, and who do not like the results of psychometric testing. Hitler banned IQ testing because he thought it was a Jewish invention (although Jews actually played less part in the development of intelligence testing than in almost any other part of psychology), and Stalin banned it because he considered it a bourgeois practice (although the motivation of the early pioneers in IQ testing was to give bright working-class children a better chance of acquiring a good education). The utter ignorance of the media is shown by the fact that I am often introduced as the 'inventor of the IQ', when IQ measurement actually preceded my birth by five years. Similarly, I have been called 'the person who showed that the IQ was inherited', when in reality this was proved long before I came into psychology, and I have never even worked in this field. It would not be sensible to take seriously criticisms made by people who have had no training in this complex field, and who simply voice their prejudices.

What is the IQ?

The notion of IQ originated from the observation that, as they grow up, children can do increasingly difficult things, solve increasingly difficult problems, learn increasingly difficult concepts and ideas. This led to the idea of *'mental age'*. Consider the very simple test in Fig. 1. The 10 drawings are shown to the child who is then asked to copy each one. The items are sequentially arranged in order of difficulty, and it is found that young children succeed only with the first one or two items, but as they get older, they are more able to copy the difficult items. This is not a function of teaching; it is practically impossible to coach young children to succeed with an item beyond their ability. Even when, by dint of hard practice, children are taught to succeed with an item beyond the usual ability for their age, they are found to forget their skill after a few days, and to return to their proper stage. This test correlates very well with other tests of intelligence, and is less influenced by cultural and environmental factors than most.

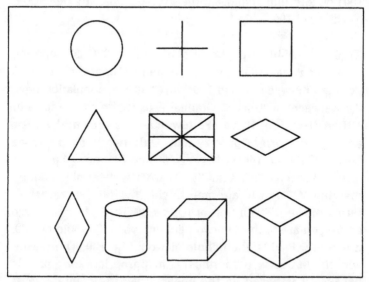

Fig. 1 Ten diagrams to be copied by a child as a measure of mental age. The older the child, the more complex the drawings he or she will be able to copy accurately.

We find that the average five-year-old can copy the first three drawings, but fails with the others. We can go on and say that the mental age (MA) of any child, whatever his or her chronological age (CA), who can copy the first three drawings but none of the others, is five years. We would not base our estimate on just one test but on a large number, but the principle is the same. To determine the child's IQ, we divide mental age by chronological age, and multiply by 100. Thus consider two children, both with a mental age of eight. The first has a chronological age of six, and accordingly an

IQ of 133 (8/6 × 100);

the other has a chronological age of twelve, and accordingly an

IQ of 67 (8/12 × 100).

High IQs (over 100) denote bright children, low IQs (below 100) denote dull* children; the average child, by definition, has an IQ of 100.

IQs are distributed roughly as shown in Fig. 2. Of all children, 25 per cent have IQs between 100 and 110, and another 25 per cent between 90 and 100; thus half the population have IQs between 90 and 110. Gradually, as we go to extremes in either direction, there are fewer and fewer children (or adults) very bright or very dull. Only two per cent score between 130 and 140, or between 60 and 70; only 0.4 per cent over 140 or under 60. Actually IQs are now determined not by dividing MA by CA, and multiplying by 100, but rather in terms of the distribution of IQs as in Fig. 2; if in your age group you are in the top two per cent, your IQ would be 130; if you are dead in the middle, it would be 100. The reason why the MA/CA x 100 formula is inappropriate for adults is because it is based on the linear growth of mental age. It works well up to the age of about 16, but there is little or no

* The word 'dull' refers to those with relatively low IQ scores. It is employed as a scientific rather than emotive term and is not meant to offend.

growth after 20. So if we used the formula, a person with an IQ of 100 at 20 years of age would have one of 50 at 40! The technicalities do not really matter; we still talk about the IQ, but we figure it out by a different formula which gives us the same result for children, but a more meaningful one for adults.

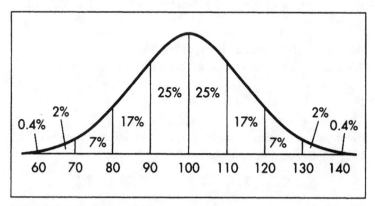

Fig. 2 The distribution of IQ in the population.

IQ Tests

What sort of tests do we use to measure the IQ? The items in this book – all of which have been specially generated on computer – will tell you. You may feel that this is a somewhat subjective procedure; how do I know that any particular item is a good measure of IQ? The answer is simply that the field is a very lawful one: any item that presents a cognitive problem correlates with any other such item. In other words, if A has a higher IQ than B, then A will tend to do better than B on any IQ item, however chosen or constructed. Thus if we give 1000 items to 1000 people, chosen at random, and measure their success, then all the items will correlate together – in other words, if you do well on one, you will be likely to do well on all the others. So up to a point you can choose your items more or less at random; you will still get a good measure.

But further than that, some types of item correlate more highly with all the tests than do other types of item. To make it a good test of IQ you would choose items of this kind, so the choice is not arbitrary, but lawful, and all good IQ tests are found to give much the same answer about a particular person's IQ.

What are 'good' items? Here are a few examples which will illustrate this concept. First we have number sequences:

$$2 \quad 4 \quad 7 \quad 11 \quad 16 \quad ?$$

The numbers increase in a regular fashion, 2, 3, 4 and 5 – so the next increase must be by 6, and the correct solution is 22. Very similar are letter sequences:

$$C \quad E \quad H \quad L \quad Q \quad ?$$

Here again letters follow the same sequence as above, so the next letter is W. Sequences can be much more complex, but the idea will be clear.

We can also have figural sequences, like this:

Select the correct figure:

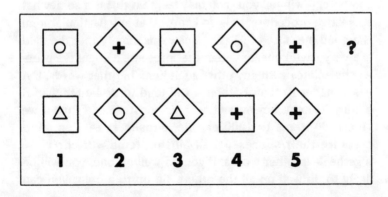

In terms of the outer figures, squares alternate with diamonds, so the next item must be a diamond on the outside. The inner figures are following the pattern nought – cross – triangle, so the next item must have a triangle on the inside. The correct answer is, therefore figure 3.

The most successful form of test item has been what is called 'matrices'. Here is an example.

Select the correct figure:

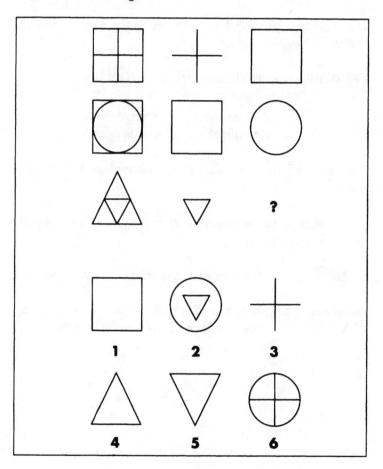

There are three figures in each line, subtract the second from the first to get the third, so 4 is the correct answer.

Somewhat different is the following question:

FINGER is to HAND as SPOKE is to:

Socket	**Speak**	**Wine**
Wheel	**Radius**	**Circle**

The relation is part to whole, so wheel is the correct answer. In a similar way:

CHURCHILL is to HITLER as WELLINGTON is to:

Alexander	**Napoleon**
Hannibal	**Montgomery**

The relation is one of opposition, so **Napoleon** is the right answer.

Incomplete sentences is another favourite. What words are missing in this sentence?:

Rome .... Carthage in the three .... wars.

History tells us that Rome **DEFEATED** Carthage in the three **PUNIC** Wars; no other words could properly fit into the gaps.

There are some additional facts to consider. The IQ measures general intelligence, but we also have special abilities. Some people of the same IQ are specially gifted verbally, some in respect of dealing with numbers, some others in relation to visuo-spatial problems as shown in Fig. 3. In this test, you are asked to draw lines in the empty outlines on the right to show how all the black figures on the left could be fitted in. An IQ test should incorporate verbal, numerical and visuo-spatial problems in roughly equal numbers.

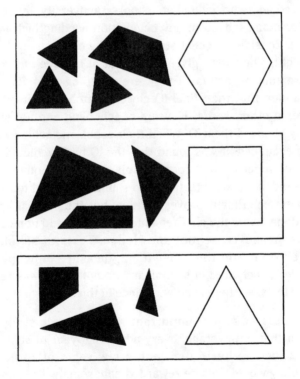

Fig. 3 Test of visuo-spatial ability.

For many purposes we might be interested in highlighting abilities, and special tests have been constructed to measure them in addition to IQ. There is more to be said about the whole business of constructing and validating IQ tests, but it is beyond the scope of this book to go into technical details.

What do IQ tests measure?

How do we know that IQ tests measure what we call intelligence, and are not just games, like crossword puzzles in the newspapers? The answer is that the scores predict who will succeed and who will fail at school, at university, in the professions, and indeed in any occupation needing high intelligence. Consider a recent study of all the children on the Isle of Wight. They were given an IQ test at the age of five, i.e. before entering school. They were tested again at 16, and it was found that their final IQ closely matched their original score; in other words, 11 years of schooling had not significantly changed their IQ. When their scholastic achievements were examined, it was found that the IQ had predicted their level of success with considerable accuracy. Some critics scoff and say that IQ tests are so similar to school tests that such an experiment proves nothing, but the original IQ test was done *before* the children entered school, and none of the items measured school knowledge. Tests of scholastic achievement, on the other hand, measure only specific knowledge acquired at school, and do not in any way resemble IQ tests, so there is no substance in this criticism.

Is success at school important? A large-scale study has shown that, on average, every additional year of schooling raises income by 16 per cent; a few years of additional schooling would thus be rewarded handsomely. IQ tests also predict fairly accurately who will do well at university where further training is available for most of the prestigious and high-income professions. Officer selection in the armed forces has found that IQ tests give invaluable help in finding suitable candidates. So, therefore, IQ is vital in doing well in life, at least financially, although it does not guarantee happiness! It does not guarantee success, either; you also need hard work, persistence, and high motivation. With a low IQ, however, these qualities do not suffice.

Interview or test?

Universities have successfully used IQ testing in their undergraduate selection procedures. This may seem remarkable, given that all candidates have good scholastic qualifications so the actual *range* of ability presented is much less than that obtaining in the population as a whole. Candidates hardly ever have an IQ below 110 or thereabouts, whereas in the general population around 75 per cent fall into that category. Such restriction of range makes selection much more difficult; where all are tall, it is most difficult to pick the tallest! Yet consider an experiment performed at the London School of Economics (LSE) at the end of the Second World War, when an unusually large number of candidates presented themselves. The usual method of selection was followed, which consisted of an interview by an experienced don, aided by a headmaster's recommendation and an essay written by the candidate. In addition, however, and for purely experimental purposes, candidates were given an IQ test, which was not taken into account in the selection process; indeed, it was not even scored until four years later when the results of the students' work was known. At this stage the relative success of the students in question was correlated with, firstly, the don's judgment and predictions and secondly, the IQ results. The outcome was very clear. The don's judgment had hardly any predictive power; indeed, when the influence of the headmaster's report and the essay was removed statistically, it had a negative value. In other words, the don chose the worse students, rather than the better ones! In contrast, the IQ test gave a good account of itself, predicting success and failure with acceptable accuracy. Despite these results, the LSE continued to use the interview technique, and rejected the IQ measure! We were never told why, but the answer is conjectural. Few people are willing to give up power and influence. The god-like don, arbitrarily admitting the candidates he or she likes, and rejecting those not liked, would fight to the death any system, however much better in objective terms, that would lessen his or her importance, power and influence.

Despite its widespread use, interviewing is not *reliable*. This term in psychology has a very definite meaning. A method, to be considered reliable, has to give similar results on repetition. If you looked at the clocks in a certain building and found that they all gave different times, you would say that these clocks were *unreliable*. Although by chance one might be right, you would not know which. Methods known to be unreliable are therefore useless; they cannot give you a veridical answer.

The inheritance of intelligence

Experts agree that differences in IQ are largely determined by heredity, and there are many different ways to investigate the point. Here I briefly list them, addressing the question of what the figures realistically mean.

Identical twins

We can study identical twins who have been separated very early in life and brought up in quite different circumstances. Several investigators have carried out such studies and the usual finding is that the twins, sharing identical genes, are very alike in IQ. It makes little difference at what age they were separated, or how different their upbringing; the overwhelming fact is their similarity.

Fraternal twins

On average, fraternal twins share only 50 per cent of genes. If IQ is largely heritable, theirs should be less alike than those of identical twins who share 100 per cent of their genes. Innumerable studies have shown that this is indeed so; roughly speaking, the similarity in IQ of fraternal twins is about half that found in identical twins.

Familial relationship

Genetics tell us that if a trait is inherited to any substantial extent, then the closeness of blood relationship in a family should predict the similarity in IQ. Thus first-degree relatives (brothers and sisters, parents and children) should have IQs as similar as those of fraternal twins. Uncles and cousins should show less similarity, and so forth. It has been found, quite universally, that this general law is obeyed for IQ.

Adoption

Adopted children derive their heredity from their biological parents, their upbringing from their adoptive parents. If adopted at birth, which influence is stronger? The answer is that their IQ resembles that of their biological parents much more than that of their adoptive parents. Interestingly enough, the longer they are with their adoptive parents, the less their IQ resembles that of their adoptive parents, and the more it resembles that of their biological parents.

Regression to the mean

It is a well-known law of genetics that any trait, physical or mental, that is determined in part by heredity will cause the children of parents who are above or below the average to regress to the population mean. Thus very tall parents have tall children, but of lesser height than the parents. Very small parents have small children, but taller than their parents. The same is true of intelligence. The children of the dull and

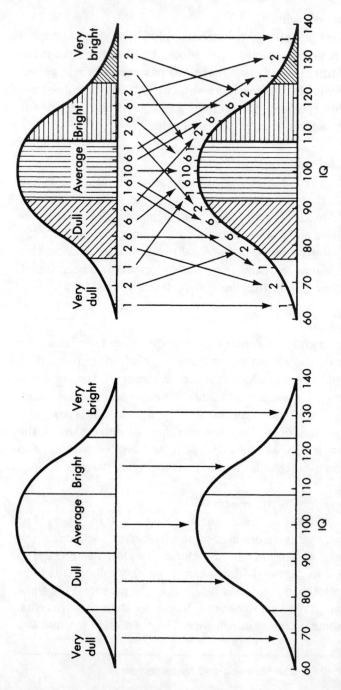

Fig. 4 The relation of parental (top) and filial (bottom) IQ. The diagram on the left illustrates what most people think happens; the diagram on the right shows what actually happens. This illustrates the law of regression to the mean.

very dull regress upwards, those of the bright and very bright downwards, and among children of average parents, some go up, some down, and some stay in the middle. UK society is socially mobile in that it does not have a caste system. It has been found that, even in the same families, the brighter offspring go up in social class, the duller go down. This is a very important social consequence of IQ being determined by genetic factors.

Inbreeding depression

Another well-known feature of genetics is that, if two related persons (such as brother and sister, father and daughter, cousin and cousin) have children, these will generally be less healthy than children of non-incestuous pairings. They will also have lower IQs than they would otherwise have had, considering the IQs of their parents.

Heterosis

The opposite of inbreeding depression, heterosis, is also sometimes known as hybrid vigour, and describes the superior heredity of offspring where the parents come from entirely different stocks, such as Caucasian and Mongoloid. Such offspring have been found to have higher IQs than they would have had if their parents had come from the same race.

Environmental factors

Semi-experimental studies have been carried out in which the possible influence of environmental factors has been decreased drastically by making the environment as identical as possible for a group of children. This was done in a study of children in an orphanage to which they were taken shortly after birth; diet, teaching, sleeping arrangements and everything else were the same for all the children. If environment was very important, then the variability of IQ should have been much less between these children than in the outside world where some children have a very good environment, others a very poor one. Yet instead of all children having the same IQ, there were bright, dull and average IQ children, just as in the world outside. Similarly, a study done in Poland looked at children whose parents earned the same amount of money, who lived in identical houses in the same environment, where schools and health provision were identical – where, in fact, communist authorities had reduced environmental differences as much as humanly possible. Yet the children differed as much in IQ as do those in capitalist countries. This is more proof of the importance of genetic factors.

IQ test items

A final argument brings together the discussion of *how* we select IQ test items, and how we measure degrees of heritability. If we had a large selection of items which measured IQ with varying amounts of success – some 'good' items, some 'mediocre', others 'poor' – then, if IQ is largely determined by genetic factors, the 'good' items should show most heritability, the 'poor' ones least, and the 'mediocre' ones intermediate. This is precisely what happens.

I have tried to describe all these experiments and their results in words, but in reality they are normally expressed in mathematical form, which makes all the arguments much more precise. Readers wishing to go further might like to consult a textbook like Nathan Brody's *Intelligence* (Academic Press, 1992). Suffice it to say that when we bring together all these different methods of estimating the heritability of intelligence, they converge on a value of about 70 per cent, leaving environment to contribute 30 per cent. There is yet more proof for the correctness of this general approach: when we measure indices of environmental determination of IQ (socioeconomic status of parents; type of schooling; number of books and journals in the house; cars, telephones, and other appliances, etc.), the overall effect falls well short of 30 per cent. In the formulae used by geneticists, measurement errors are counted as part of the environmental effects, so that 70 per cent is probably an underestimate of the genetic determination of IQ in our society. So environment matters, but much less so than heredity.

It is necessary to qualify this estimate of IQ heritability because heritability is not an absolute quality, like the speed of light; it is a population statistic which describes a particular population at a particular time. A good comparison would be height. The average height of Englishmen at the moment is about 5 feet 10 inches (1.78 metres). That of Japanese men is more like 5 feet 8 inches (1.73 metres). But Englishmen 300 years ago were, if anything, smaller than Japanese men now, and Japanese in the USA are as tall as Englishmen now. Yet height is very heritable, much more so than IQ! What is heritable is the cause of variation in a given population; what determines differences *between* populations may be something entirely different, like nutrition in the case of height.

Consider a Norwegian study investigating the heritability of school achievement. (In so far as school achievement is due to high IQ, to that extent it should be heritable.) The school system in Norway has changed considerably from just after the Second World War to the early 1980s when the study was carried out, becoming much more egalitarian. The more egalitarian the system, the less the influence of environment, and consequently it was predicted that heritability of school achievement should increase – which it did. You can always increase the influence of environment by reducing a child's opportunity to learn. If you bring the child up in a dark cellar, without real human intercourse, and without any teaching, the child will grow up permanently damaged in his or her ability to think – the so-called Kaspar Hauser Syndrome, named after one such unfortunate child. The heritability value of 70 per cent is therefore not absolute; it is simply characteristic of present-day western society, and might not apply to Indian society at the moment, where it is probably lower, or to English society 300 years ago, where it was probably also lower.

Some of the methods demonstrating the heritability of IQ have been criticized. It has been suggested, for example, that the comparison of identical and fraternal twins assumes that identical twins are not treated more similarly than fraternal twins; if they were, then their greater similarity in intelligence (and in personality) might be due to this treatment. It is true that identical twins are treated more similarly than fraternal twins, often being given the same clothes, hair-cuts and so on. Such treatment, however, is quite irrelevant to a person's IQ, and when measured and taken into account, it made no difference to the outcome – identical twins were still much more alike in IQ than fraternal twins. Another demonstration of this is that parents are sometimes wrong in identifying their children as identical or fraternal. Children misidentified in this manner behave just as they should in terms of their true relationship; fraternal twins mistakenly thought to be identical by their parents are much less alike in IQ than identical twins thought to be fraternal.

When we turn to identical twins separated early in life, it is often pointed out that the circumstances in which they are brought up may not be all that different – the adoptive parents may be similar to the biological parents in respect to their socioeconomic status. There are two answers to this argument. Firstly, we can measure the importance of socioeconomic status by looking at cousins; they share socioeconomic status to an even greater extent than separated identical twins, yet their correlation for IQ is only about .19, part (or all) of which is due to their genetic similarity, leaving very little effectiveness for the socioeconomic factor. The other answer is to look for IQ similarity when the effects of socioeconomic influence are removed statistically; there is very little change. When the influence of genetic factors is removed, however, nothing is left. If there is any influence of socioeconomic factors, it cannot be at all strong.

To me, the most important argument for the validity of the 70 per cent heredity – 30 per cent environment estimate is this: all the different methods of estimating heritability, and they are very different indeed, agree on the estimate. If they were all beset with (different) serious errors, this would be an extremely unlikely outcome. It is simply unbelievable that such agreement could be produced by compensating errors. Indeed, no expert believes anything of the kind; they all agree that the heritability of IQ is one of the most firmly established facts in psychology, although minor differences and questions still remain. There are still questions about the number of genes involved in creating IQ differences, for instance, and it will be a long time before we can expect to locate them. But that does not affect the argument. We do not know everything about the inheritance of the IQ, but we do know enough to be sure of the fact that it has a substantial heritability.

The biological basis of IQ

There is an important deduction to be made from the fact that IQ is strongly determined by genetic factors. Clearly the genes cannot influence behaviour directly – and doing an IQ test is behaviour. There must be biological mechanisms (physiological, hormonal) which mediate between DNA, the

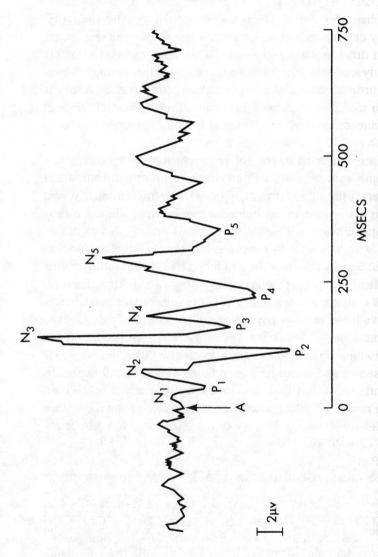

Fig. 5 An illustration of the evoked potential on the electroencephalogram (EEG).

genetic material, and IQ, and recent years have seen many attempts to look for such intermediaries. The most important so far has been the discovery that the electroencephalogram (EEG), which records brain waves, can successfully discriminate between the wave characteristics of bright and dull children. Most successful has been a type of EEG study known as the averaged evoked potential (AEP) which records what happens in the cortex during the transmission of a message. Fig. 5 shows on the left the ordinary EEG meandering along, until at point A a signal is given – a single flash of light or a tone. This produces a series of large waves which subside after 500 milliseconds. The successive negative and positive peaks are numbered, or may be referred to by the time they occur after the signal is given; thus we talk about the P300, meaning a positive peak occurring after about 300 milliseconds.

Figs. 6 and 7 show the resulting patterns of wave forms, after auditory and visual signals respectively, for six bright and six dull children (their IQs are shown on the vertical axes). The wave-forms are clearly quite different, being much more complex for the bright children. A simple wave-form consists of two or three major ups and downs, with a few superimposed peaks and troughs. A complex wave-form, on the other hand, has large numbers of these peaks and troughs. There are now good theories to tell us *why* there should be such differences.

AEP studies have a very poor signal-to-noise ratio, so that to get a meaningful pattern we have to perform the experiment 100 times or so and *average* the evoked potentials. Such averaging assumes that we observe identical events each time the AEP is being measured, but that may not always be so. During the transmission of a message through the cortex, i.e., from the dendrites of one cell through the intermediary

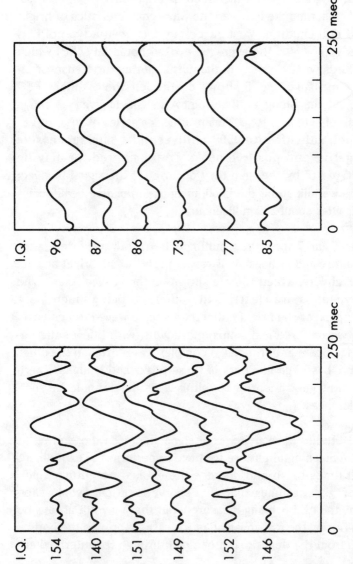

Fig. 6 Evoked potential waveforms for six high and six low IQ subjects, following auditory stimulation.

I.Q.			I.Q.		
154			96		
140			87		
151			86		
149			73		
152			77		
146			85		

0   250 msec   0   250 msec

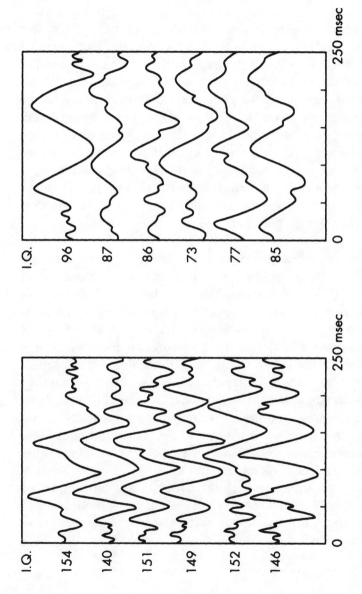

Fig. 7 Evoked potential waveforms for six high and six low IQ subjects, following visual stimulation.

of the synapse to the axons of other cells, *errors* may occur that alter the EEG picture. Thus to obtain some of the smaller peaks and troughs, every (or nearly every) one of the 100 records taken must show a peak or a trough at the same point; that means *errorless* transmission of the message. Now imagine that a large number of errors occurs. At a given point we might have a trough on one occasion, a peak on another occasion, and neither a peak nor a trough on a third. That would even out all the peaks and troughs except the two or three major waves. In other words, errors in transmission through the cortex would produce exactly the effect we are looking for, i.e. the smoothing out of all the minor features that produce the complexity of the records characteristic of the bright children. And if such errors occur they would be expected to make problem solution more difficult, and thus account for the low IQ of the dull.

Where can these errors occur? The most obvious place is the synapse, where the message contained in the dendrites of one cell is handed over to the axon of another. This is a very complex process, in which the electrical form of transmission typical of axons and dendrites is changed to the chemical forms typical of the synapse. Another candidate is myelin – the insulating agent of the axons and dendrites, which protects the integrity of the electrical transmission; this sheath may have thin patches or holes, breaking down the insulation and causing errors. A third possibility is that dull children have shorter dendrites than bright ones have, making proper connections difficult. (It has been found that dendrite length correlates with IQ, and that as intelligence-test performance declines with old age, so dendrites shorten.) Any of these, or all three, may be active to produce the errors in transmission that characterize the records of dull children.

Another way to look at the hypothesis of an ill-functioning cortical system is to think of the consequences of having the tuning of your car engine badly adjusted, or some other faulty functioning of the engine. One consequence is that, compared with a well-functioning engine of equal capacity, the badly functioning engine will use more petrol. It seems that if the cortex of a dull person is malfunctioning, as suggested, then it would use more fuel than that of a bright person for identical work. The fuel for the brain is glucose, and it is possible to relate glucose uptake by the brain as a consequence of doing a specified cognitive task, such as an IQ test. This can be done using the PET scan (positron emission tomography). Results show that total glucose uptake is negatively correlated with IQ, indicating that, as predicted, error-prone brains need more fuel.

The theory of errors in transmission can be tested in yet another way. AEP waves have greater amplitude when novel stimuli are applied; this indicates greater attention being paid to novel stimuli. What happens when identical stimuli are repeatedly presented to the subject? The amplitude of the AEP waves declines, *but less so for dull than for bright subjects*. This is as expected; identical stimuli, to be so classified, have to be perceived without error. If error-transmissions are involved, they may not appear identical, and hence produce greater amplitude AEP waves.

There is now a good deal of evidence to suggest that the general theory of high IQ being linked with error-free processing of information through the cortex is along the right lines, although much more research is needed to nail it down completely, discover the precise locus of these 'errors', and if possible measure them directly – the AEP is a very indirect method for doing it.

Can we increase IQ?

There have been many attempts to increase IQ by providing special teaching, better housing, improved parenting – all to little avail. In many cases success has been very transitory – specially coached children succeed better as far as school achievement and IQ tests are concerned, but as they grow older they fall back to their original level. What is often done is to 'teach the test'; in other words, children are taught how to do the tests they will be given (directly or indirectly). They do well on the tests they have been taught, but this does not generalize to their school performance as a whole. The literature in this area is very disappointing, characterized by excessive claims, poor methodology and worse statistics. The comparative failure of the American 'head start' programme is one illustration. This was a government initiative costing about a billion dollars. The aim was to equip schools to give special educational support to deprived children in the hope that their IQs and scholastic performance might improve.

There is one exception to the general rule that not much can be done to raise a child's IQ. It has been found that many children, although given what appears to be a perfectly adequate diet, eat too many sweets and 'junk' foods, and too little fruit and vegetables. Their intake of vitamins and minerals is low, although not sufficiently so to attract medical attention. When given vitamin and mineral supplementation, however, their IQ increases markedly. Studies have taken large groups of apparently well-fed children and divided them into control groups, which are given placebo pills, and treatment groups, which are given proper supplementation. The treatment group achieves a four-point IQ advantage over the placebo group on average. This may not seem much, but the supplementation does nothing for most children who have a sufficiently high level of vitamins and minerals; it helps only those who do suffer from a deficiency. (You can determine who is suffering from a dietary deficiency by taking and analysing blood samples.) For such children, an average increase in IQ of 11 points has been recorded.

These were well-fed children, by any ordinary standards; an even better effect could be expected if the supplementation were given to children suffering serious dietary deficiency. It is typical of our society and its dislike of genetic and biological causes of human behaviour that (literally!) billions of dollars have been wasted on unsuccessful environmental attempts to raise IQ, while no money is available to continue the research into biological causes.

There are two further facts concerning dietary supplementation which are of interest. The first is that, as one might have expected, the effects on IQ are largest for the youngest group (10 points on average for six-year-olds) and smallest for the oldest (one point for 18-year-olds). The second is that effects seem to last for at least a year, longer periods have not been investigated as yet.

Different Intelligences?

So far I have talked about IQ, rather than about intelligence. The reason is simply that intelligence is a word used in many different ways and contexts, and that without clarification one can easily get into misunderstandings and unnecessary arguments. Consider Fig. 8, which portrays the relation between three different conceptions of intelligence. We can talk about *biological intelligence*, as measured for instance by the evoked potential. This is almost completely determined by genetic factors. Differences in this biological intelligence are largely responsible for differences in *psychometric intelligence* (IQ), but there are also important cultural, educational, familial and socioeconomic determinants. Finally we have

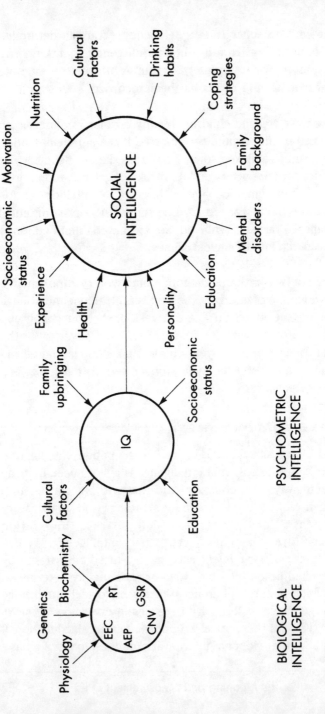

Fig. 8 Different notions of 'intelligence' – biological, psychometric and social.

social or practical intelligence, referring to what we do with our IQ. Here there is a host of external determinants to influence the way we use our IQ. If we drink too much alcohol we may fail, although our IQ is high enough to succeed. If we suffer from neurotic symptoms, we may throw away all our intellectual advantages. Our personality may predispose us to laziness, lack of motivation, and other causes of failure. There are too many of these factors to name them all; some are noted in the figure.

A few words may be said here concerning social or practical intelligence because critics have often pointed out that many people with low IQ's are highly successful materially, while some with high IQ's are unsuccessful. The phrase often heard is: 'If you're so clever why ain't you rich?' The most obvious answer is that you may value other things more highly than money. To a scientist, an artist, or a religious person truth, beauty and goodness are vastly more important than money. It is absurd to regard being rich as *the* measure of success. The most intelligent may see through the shallowness of worldly success. Another important point is that there are many other qualities than IQ which are valued by the crowd. The highest rewards may go to successful sportsmen and sportswomen; to entertainers; to film stars; to jazz singers and musicians; to models; to royalty – indeed, there is a long list of people of very ordinary intelligence who earn hundreds of times the amount earned by Einstein, or Schubert, or Van Gogh. On the whole, however, those who earn much money are fairly bright, and those who are dull seldom become rich, but we would be foolish to expect a one-to-one relation. For many, being gifted is its own reward.

Speed v. Power

Items used in IQ testing can be divided into two great classes, sometimes called *speed* and *power* tests. A power test would be one so difficult that many people would not succeed with it however long they took over it. Here the criterion of success would be whether the problem was successfully solved or not. Speed tests, on the other hand, are relatively easy, so that just about everyone can solve the problems involved. Here success is measured in terms of the speed of solution. For a speed test, one sets a given time limit, say 30 minutes, and supplies more items than even the brightest can solve in the time given; the score is the number successfully completed in that time.

These are extremes; most tests combine the two types of items. It used to be thought that they measure two different types of intelligence: profound (power tests) and superficial (speed tests). The facts seem to contradict this attractive notion; experiment shows that speed of thinking underlies success of both types of test equally. If your thought processes are very slow, your chances of ever solving a complex problem vanish because by the time you get around to considering one aspect, you have forgotten the others. Speed is important because the number of ideas we can hold in short-term memory is severely restricted, and if we are slow in dealing with them, they disappear. Speed of cognitive processing seems to be a fundamental feature underlying success in IQ determination.

Knowledge-testing v. problem-solving

Rather more important is another distinction which may be made in IQ items, namely that of knowledge-testing versus problem-solving. It may denote either capacity for learning and problem-solving, or possession of a large amount of acquired knowledge. Many IQ tests use vocabulary items, such as this:

			Which of these
MUNIFICENCE:	1	Mummification	**four words means**
	2	Monstrosity	**the same as**
	3	Generosity	**munificence ?**
	4	Garrulity	

To answer this question, you must know the meaning of the words involved. This is quite a different task to that involved in the test items given on an earlier page, where no special knowledge is required to solve the problems in question. In psychology, we have the distinction between *fluid* and *crystallized* intelligence. Fluid intelligence is measured by items such as sequences and matrices; no special knowledge is required, and you use your intelligence to solve the problem in a novel sort of way. Fluid intelligence enables you to acquire knowledge, such as knowledge of words; thus fluid intelligence becomes crystallized as special knowledge. Both can be used to measure IQ in homogeneous populations, because in such populations everyone has had much the same chance to use his or her fluid intelligence to acquire crystallized knowledge. But for anyone coming from a different culture or sub-culture crystallized knowledge items may not be a fair test of his or her fluid intelligence; hence although both are highly correlated in our society, psychologists prefer for the most part to use tests of fluid ability.

Sometimes the two are combined, as in the following:

HIGH is to LOW as BIG is to:

short, small, stout, great

Here practically everyone would know the words, and hence this is mostly a test of fluid ability, i.e. the ability to extract the relation of <u>opposite</u> and apply it to the right side of the equation. But consider an item having exactly the same form:

Odysseus is to Penelope as Menelaus is to:
Circe, Helen, Narsicaa, Artemis, Eros

This is an almost pure test of knowledge. If you know that Penelope was Odysseus's wife and that Helen was Menelaus's wife, the answer is clear. If you know neither, then no amount of fluid ability will enable you to find the answer.

If fluid tests of ability are better and purer measures of intelligence, why should we ever want to use crystallized tests? There are two good reasons. Crystallized ability can be tested much more quickly than fluid ability; a short vocabulary test will get you a good approximation in five minutes, and if an approximation to the true IQ will do, you will have more time for other investigation. The second point is more important, and more complicated. Often an IQ test is used for a practical purpose, and you want it to be as *predictive* as possible, regardless of its effectiveness as a *pure* measure of IQ. Let us say that you want to predict a child's success at school, or a student's success at university. A high score on a test involving crystallized ability will tell you that the student has high fluid ability (or he/she could not have acquired that much knowledge), but for success at school or university, other qualities are required as well, such as motivation, persistence and application. Hence you may prefer to use a test that is not a pure measure of IQ, but which gives you a combined measure of fluid ability and relevant personality factors. It has been found that such an impure test is actually more predictive than a pure test of fluid ability; it might be even better to measure both aspects separately, and then combine them in the most predictive manner. That takes time, however, and may not be possible for administrative reasons.

Education and IQ

Children have failed examinations for thousands of years; now we often blame the psychologist who measures their IQ and finds it low for their failure! The limitations of human intelligence, and its variability, are not due to the psychologists who set out to make their measurement more accurate. We now know much more about Cicero's *intelligentia* than he did, but even then it was well known that some people are bright, others dull, with only a few outstanding in their mental abilities.

Does this knowledge in fact help us in any way to improve our educational system? Does it keep us from making elementary errors in organizing the education of our children? Can we use the knowledge given us by the kind of research I have been describing? The answer is a resounding 'Yes', provided that we do not let political prejudice override the verdict of science. In what follows I will illustrate this general proposition.

My first example is the diagnosis of *overachievement*. We know fairly well what the scholastic achievement should be of children at various IQ levels. Some clearly do much better than that; they are *overachievers*. Of course they do not present any problem; they have studied hard, paid attention to their teachers, concentrated in class, done all their homework, and have spent additional time and energy working out problems, doing additional reading, and writing essays beyond the call of duty. Some critics have said scornfully that if IQ determines levels of scholastic achievement, there cannot be such a thing as overachievement – how can you achieve more than your IQ level allows? This is nonsense; nobody ever suggested that IQ and scholastic achievement were *perfectly* correlated, and that other factors played no part. Hard work, high motivation to do well, persistence –

these are also vitally important, and may lead a child to do well in spite of a relatively low level of intelligence.

More important from the therapeutic point of view is the chronic *underachiever*. Why does Johnny, with his IQ of 140, do so poorly, given his high intelligence? We only know that he is an underachiever because we can measure his IQ, and it is the discrepancy between potential and actual achievement that alerts us to the existence of a problem. Having diagnosed the *problem*, we may go on to try and find an answer. Remember that we would never have searched for the answer in the absence of the IQ measurement. We would simply have said: Johnny is doing badly, so presumably Johnny is rather dull. But his high IQ shows that this reasoning is faulty, so what ails Johnny?

I encountered this question shortly after I was appointed psychologist to the Maudsley Hospital. An irate high-level civil servant had complained to the school where his son was apparently battling unsuccessfully to keep up with his classmates. He claimed that his son was very bright, and that bad teaching was responsible. The school asserted that there was nothing wrong with their teaching, but that the boy was just unable to learn properly. Johnny had been referred to the children's department at the Maudsley, which was in charge of a hard-bitten old Freudian who recommended long-term psychoanalysis to unravel Johnny's Oedipus complex, a suggestion that did not appeal to me. Surreptitiously I gave Johnny an IQ test, which revealed an IQ of 145; the father had been right about his child's intelligence. Why had he failed scholastically? I noticed that when he looked at me, his eyes creased up a bit, suggesting that he might be short-sighted. I gave him a rough Snellen Chart test, and found that he was very short-sighted indeed. He was prescribed glasses, and soared ahead at school to end up top of his class. I went on to test the whole class and found two other boys who were underachievers; both of them had moderately severe hearing defects, which were cleared up medically.

However bright you are, if you cannot see what the teacher writes on the board, or hear what the teacher says, you are not going to keep up with the rest of the class. There are many thousands of children in Britain, handicapped without knowing it, or without anyone realizing it, who are underachievers, and who would be helped, if only regular IQ testing were introduced in all schools. Teachers in the usual large classes judge children's intelligence by their performance; they seldom spot underachievers. It needs an objective measure of IQ to ring the alarm bells. Of course not all problems posed by underachievers are remedied so easily, but it is nearly always possible to help the child.

Teachers sometimes object to IQ testing because of what is sometimes called the 'Pygmalion Effect'. In 1968, Rosenthal and Jacobson published a book, *Pygmalion in the Classroom*, in which they tried to prove that low performance of pupils on IQ tests resulted from teachers' expectations; these in turn would come from considerations of the pupil's race or social class, and other sociological and biological background variables. This hypothesis has achieved wide acceptance, and if true would tend to discredit IQ testing, and with it the whole theory of intelligence supported by so much evidence in this book. The evidence presented, however, does not support the conclusion reached. All the major critical reviewers of the study on which the hypothesis is based have pointed to vital faults and errors in its design and analysis. Since then, dozens of studies have been done in an attempt to replicate this work but none have succeeded in finding any evidence for the Pygmalion effect! These studies were inifinitely superior to the original Rosenthal and

Jacobson one in point of technique, controls and measurement.

IQ testing is relevant to much broader educational issues, such as the very practice of education itself. It used to be taken for granted that teaching was most effective in classes where children were of roughly similar ability; thus the brightest were educated in the British grammar school, or else the so-called public schools, the German Gymnasium, or the French lycée. This system produced a high level of scholastic achievement among the bright; it also ensured a reasonable level among the not-so-bright who would not have managed to keep up with the high-IQ elite, but who received the best education suitable for their mental abilities. There was little illiteracy, and little innumeracy; even the dullest emerged with sufficient ability to read and write, and do elementary arithmetic. Almost all were employable.

There were of course many injustices. Very bright working-class children often failed to obtain higher-education for which their talents fitted them; selection on the basis of scholastic achievement did not do their abilities justice because their primary education was nothing like as good as that offered to their middle-class peers.

It was this injustice that motivated the pioneers of IQ testing in England and Scotland to urge for IQ tests to take the place of achievement tests in the selection process for grammar schools and university. Their basis was that IQ tests were much less vulnerable to environmental handicaps. Selection became much more accurate as a result, responding to a child's innate ability rather than his or her earlier educational advantages. Proof came when a Labour government introduced the system of comprehensive schools and abolished selection; immediately the proportion of working-class children in higher education fell drastically and for many years the standard of scholastic achievement in British schools dropped alarmingly. Finally, even the authors of this disaster came to realize what was happening, and asked for a reassessment. Slowly efforts are being made to go back to sound educational practices, to abandon mixed ability classes, and even to reintroduce selection and grading although IQ testing is still regarded with distrust.

It should not take an intellectual giant to see that mixed ability teaching is a hopeless endeavour. Teaching such a class means trying to reach some bright, some dull, and some middling children at the same time; yet the bright will understand what you are saying the first time round; the middling bright will need repetition; and the dull will require special teaching. This means that the bright get excessively bored by the repetition needed for the rest, lose interest, play truant, or get up to all sorts of tricks. Worst of all, they lose motivation, and school becomes boring. At the other end, the dull are put off by the lack of specialized teaching that alone would make them understand. They become discouraged, note the difference between their achievements and those of the bright pupils, and begin to hate school, and all it stands for. They become undisciplined, and may make teaching and learning impossible by their behaviour. All children benefit by the system of equal-ability classes, and none lose out. Go against nature's laws, and all children will suffer – as indeed they have done over the past 30 years.

Intelligence and creativity

In thinking about intelligence, always bear in mind that human beings are not unidimensional. High or low intelligence always appears as an attribute of a human being, and its applications are therefore qualified by the general attributes of that being. Intelligence is not the abstract, ideal, arcane, recondite intellectual construct that appears in the scientific context; science always and inevitably abstracts from the blooming, buzzing confusion of everyday life. That is its strength and its weakness. In everyday life we never encounter pure intelligence; it is always associated with historical baggage, acquired knowledge, varied attitudes, divergent beliefs, emotional hang-ups. Such assemblages can be studied, but they are much more complex to analyse than intelligence pure and simple.

Consider creativity. Is creativity identical with intelligence? All the measures of IQ we have considered so far, and all the measures of IQ we present in the tests in this book, are what is called *convergent*; in other words, all the relations between the elements within a test item converge on one and only one answer. Take the series:

10   12   14   16   18   ?

The series increases by 2 each time, so it converges on the answer: 20. However, there are also *divergent* test items, and tests made up of such items measure a rather different aspect of intelligence we may call *creativity*. The essential nature of such tests implies that they are open-ended; there are many, perhaps an infinite number, of possible answers. Consider the following: How many uses can you think of for a brick? The more creative person will think of more (fluency) and more unusual (originality) types of uses. Common answers, such as 'To break a window', or 'To hit somebody over the head' are not very original. Unusual answers might be 'For a small actor to stand on when kissing a tall girl', or 'To put in an empty suitcase you are leaving in your hotel room when you leave without paying, to give the impression that the suitcase is full' might be considered rather more original.

There are many other questions you might ask: 'List as many consequences as you can of the sudden abolition of the force of gravity?' would be one. 'What would happen if we all had identical IQs?' would be another. Or you could show your subjects a picture and ask what might have happened there, or ask them to write down symbolic equivalents to certain stimuli, such as the notion of a liner departing to which they might reply 'a bird leaving England in the autumn'. The list of possible items is endless. What do they measure?

They do not measure intelligence as defined by convergent tests. There is little correlation, and tests of divergent ability hang together in a way that they do not with tests of convergent ability. Do they then measure creativity? They correlate quite well with ratings of creativity made by people who know the subjects well, and also with evidence of creativity shown at school, university or in life. When administered at school, they predict with some accuracy creativity shown in later life. Many of these correlations are reasonably high, almost as high as a teacher's rating of the IQs of his pupils, so clearly there is suggestive evidence that these tests measure at least some aspects of creativity.

There are other types of divergent test items, such as measures of word association. Here the experimenter says a word, and the subject responds as quickly as possible with another word that comes into his mind. Some responses are obvious, others less so, and some quite unique. Typical variations in reactions to two words, FOOT and COMMAND, are shown below. The responses obtained, and the number of subjects making each response, are shown. To the word FOOT, 232 people replied 'shoe(s)', but only one person replied 'dog', or 'hat', or 'rat'! If we use a list of 100 words, we can see for each respondent how popular each of his or her responses was by consulting a table containing the responses given by 1000 randomly selected people (not all responses are listed). We may then count the number of unusual responses, and see whether this correlates with objective indices of creativity.

FOOT

Shoe(s)
(232)

Hand	**Toe**	**Leg**
(198)	**(191)**	**(118)**

Soldier,	**Ball,**	**Walks,**	**Amble,**	**Arm,**	**Sore,**	**Inch(es)**
(26)	**(23)**	**(14)**	**(13)**	**(10)**	**(9)**	**(8)**

Rat, Snow, Person, Physics, Dog, Mule, Wall, Shin, Wash, Hat, End.
(singles)

COMMAND

Order
(196)

Army	**Obey**	**Officer**
(102)	**(78)**	**(65)**

Performance	**Do**	**Tell**	**Shout**	**Halt**	**Voice**	**Soldier**
(33)	**(27)**	**(27)**	**(26)**	**(23)**	**(20)**	**(18)**

Hat, Polite, Plea, Book, Salute, Fulfil, Obedience, War, Stern,
(singles)

One such experiment tested a large number of well-known American architects. Each had been rated by a panel of architects as to his or her creativity. All were highly intelligent; but they differed considerably with respect to their rated creativity. These ratings correlated quite well with their word association scores – the more creative they were, the more unusual their word associations!

Why should there be such correlations? Let us consider what creativity really means. We all acquire countless facts, ideas and notions which experience has taught us to associate in various ways. Tables and chairs are usually found together, as are feet and shoes, salt and pepper. To be creative we have to form meaningful association between *unlikely* ideas, or at least unusual ones. One inventor patented a condom that played a tune when pressure was put on the rubber ring at the top – an unusual association of ideas!

We may postulate that there is in our mind an *associative gradient*. If this is steep any given idea will produce only very closely associated ideas, and we will be *rigid* in our thinking. If the gradient is sloping gently it will take in quite remote associations, thus producing optimal conditions for creativity. The word-association test clearly measures this associative gradient; hence it correlates with true creativity, as shown by the creative architects.

But creativity must also have *social relevance* to be truly creative; the word salad produced by a schizophrenic may be full of unusual associations, but it is not truly creative in the social sense. Hence for true creativity much more is required than divergent thinking ability, or a gently sloping associative gradient. We rightly value Edison and his inventions more highly than the inventor of the musical condom, precisely because of the greater social relevance of his inventions. Similarly a social judgment, usually by his peers, decides on a judgment of 'genius'; such a judgment may be delayed for hundreds of years, but usually the greatness of our leading composers, dramatists, painters, scientists, mathematicians, and poets will eventually be recognized.

We have discussed the importance of looking for biological intermediaries between DNA and intelligence; can we discover such intermediaries also between DNA and creativity? There may be a suggestion of where to look in the fact that genius has often been linked with madness (psychosis), such as in Dryden's famous couplet:

> *Great wits are sure to madness near alli'd,*
> *And thin partitions do their bounds divide.*

There is no doubt that historically many geniuses were mad, at least at times, or were sufficiently abnormal psychologically to have the fact noted. Among modern poets, writers and scientists, too, psychopathology well above the average has been observed, often manic-depressive insanity. And the link between creativity and psychopathology has been confirmed by repeated findings that close relatives of psychotic patients are often unusually creative. So perhaps we should look at the cognitive peculiarities of psychotics for a clue?

The major cognitive characteristic of schizophrenics is what has often been called 'overinclusiveness'; in other words, they include allusions and associations in their thinking and talking that to the normal person seem completely irrelevant. This tendency also appears in their word associations, which are very unusual. In this they resemble the creative person, as we have already seen. Thus psychotic individuals appear to have the same sloping associative gradients as creative people, only more so; their associations are even more remote than those of creative individuals. Now there is good evidence that psychotic overinclusiveness is caused by an abundance of the neurotransmitter dopamine, and a relative absence of the neurotransmitter serotonin. Experimental studies have shown that administering dopamine agonists increases tendencies toward overinclusiveness, while administration of antagonists has the opposite effect. This is not the right place to discuss these findings in detail, but they do suggest a common cause for psychosis and creativity.

The qualities of genius

We all worship genius, whether in science, the arts, among statesmen and women, or anywhere we can find it. Catherine Cox examined the lives of 301 acknowledged geniuses to estimate their IQ, and came up with the *average* figure of 160! Again, a high IQ may be a necessary but is certainly not a sufficient condition for genius; there are many men and women with an IQ of 160, none of whom is a genius. IQ is predictive wherever intelligence plays a part, but other factors always play a part too.

What does the genius need, then, apart from high intelligence and high creativity? Clearly if creativity implies an associative gradient that slopes gently to give access to large numbers of remote ideas, these ideas have to be *acquired* in the first place, so hard work, motivation and great persistence are needed. If you do not have two ideas to rub together, you are not going to have enough fodder for your creativity to produce anything worthwhile. Next, circumstances have to be right; Einstein would not have prospered in an igloo, or Mozart in a kraal, or Shakespeare in a wigwam! Thus the trait of creativity is a necessary but not a sufficient ingredient of genius; very much like intelligence, genius cannot do without it, but by itself it is not enough to produce works of genius.

Is it true that there is enough agreement in the social judgment of peers to properly define a genius? Members of four of the most famous American symphony orchestras were asked to grade 17 of the most frequently played great composers, plus two less renowned modern ones (McDowell and Victor Herbert). Their judgments were remarkably consistent, and are shown in Fig. 9. It is not suggested that Haydn is necessarily a greater composer than Debussy, or Mendelssohn than

---

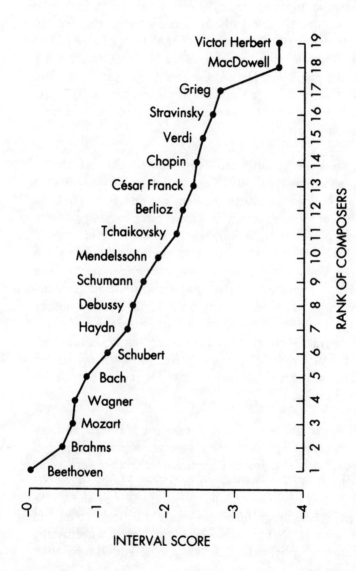

Fig. 9 Comparative rating of 19 composers by members of four famous American symphony orchestras.

Tchaikovsky, but in general few experts would disagree with the placing of Beethoven, Brahms, Mozart, Wagner and Bach at the top of the list, and Grieg, Stravinsky, Verdi, Chopin and Berlioz at the lower end, with MacDowell and Victor Herbert nowhere. One can always argue that it is unfair to compare a great composer of operas, like Verdi, with a great composer of Lieder, like Schubert; clearly one could go into endless detail and argument. Yet over the centuries there has been overwhelming agreement on who are the great composers, painters, scientists; there may be some degree of fuzziness about the definition of 'genius', but there is enough agreement to make the notion scientifically viable.

IQ and equality

One last word must be said concerning the belief held by many people, including some psychologists, that no further research should be done into socially sensitive issues such as the inheritance of intelligence, racial and social-class differences in IQ, or educational inequality. Some even go further and maintain that such issues are so socially divisive that a curtain of silence should be drawn across all that is known about them. Unfortunately we cannot make problems go away by refusing to study or discuss them. Victorians refused to discuss sex, or permit scientific studies of it; this did not prevent sex from playing an important part in their lives. Many people refuse to discuss death, but death comes to us all. We will not eliminate the threat of cancer by refusing to talk about it, or study it; quite the opposite. In the same way, psychologists have not *created* the problems posed by the inheritance of intelligence, or the observed differences between races and classes; they have merely given them a quantitative dimension. Problems of differential ability in the classroom were recognized long before modern psychology or mental testing were thought of; witness this moving quotation from the great Swiss educationalist Pestalozzi:

> It is God himself who gave rise to the inequality of men through the inequality of the talents which He hath bestowed on them; with fatherly love and wisdom He hath distributed them among His children, and we must with human love and wisdom use and accomplish what with divine love and wisdom He hath founded.

Undoubtedly the facts are sombre enough when regarded from the point of view of egalitarians from Rousseau and Locke onwards; but this is no good reason for dissimulating, or burying them in silence. As Robbie Burns once said: 'Facts are chiels that winna ding, an' downa be disputed.' (Facts are things that cannot be manipulated or disputed.) On the other hand, from the biological point of view, human diversity is an unqualified blessing; it is our safeguard and standby in times of change. How boring and deadly would human life be if we were indeed all alike! I think we must take our stand with Thomas Jefferson, the great democrat, when he said 'There is no truth existing which I fear, or would wish unknown to the whole world.'

Part Two:

Testing your IQ

In the main body of this book there are eight separate tests of your IQ. Each has 40 separate items, and each test should be timed for 30 minutes. The correct answers are given at the end of the book, so you can check how many you got right. Also at the end is a graph to enable you to translate your score into an IQ. Try to get someone else to time you; people are notoriously generous in timing themselves!

In doing the test, try each item, but if you feel you will not be able to do a particular one go on to the next; they are not in order of difficulty. Check your answer; you may be on the right track, but have made a mistake in figuring it out or in writing it down. There are some letter sequences; it may be useful if in advance you write down the letters of the alphabet, to help you count the position in a sequence. Have a pencil and a piece of paper ready to do your calculations.

The test will give you an *approximate* idea of what your IQ is; do not take it too seriously. Above all the tests are meant to give you an idea of how IQ test items are constructed, how to do the tests, how to score them. It may help you if in the future you are called upon to do a test in a selection situation where the results matter. Self-testing is not recommend - ed when the result is important; if you want a very accurate figure you should have an experienced psychologist give you an individual test. Note that performance usually improves by repetition. Your score is likely to rise from the first test to later ones as you become test-wise, i.e., you learn just what is required, how to attack different items, how to time yourself, etc. There will be obvious chance differences between the tests – you may get stuck on an item in one test, but quickly solve a similar item in another.

If you are under 18, you can still do the tests, but the transformation of scores into an IQ does not work. The younger you are, the higher your IQ for a given score, but as the tests have not been standardized on children, no exact formula can be given. Wait until you grow up. Above all, enjoy the tests like you would a crossword puzzle. The very fact that you bought the book suggests that your IQ is above 100 – few people with low IQs are interested in mental testing or buy books of this kind! If you have to do a mental test, having done these tests will above all give you confidence in knowing what sort of thing is required, and how to set about giving it your best shot.

Examples

Before starting on the tests you might like to look through these examples to see the kind of format the problems present. This will make it easier for you to get down to solving the problem, without having to think too much about the way it is presented. Bear in mind that the series and sequences can come in many different forms, and not all of these can be shown in the examples.

1:   Insert missing letter.

A   C   E   G

Answer: I. Add 2 to each letter.

2:   Underline the two phrases that are the closest in meaning.

(a)   **In the doghouse.**

(b)   **In hot water.**

(c)   **In no time.**

(d)   **In between two stools.**

Answer: a and b.

3:   Insert the missing word.

13	18	(FARM)	1	6
20	15	(CLOT)	12	3

Answer: CLOT.
Each number represents each letter position in the alphabet.

4:   Insert the missing word.

B + (hurry) = (sweep)

Answer: **(Brush)**. B + rush = BRUSH.

5:   Insert the word that is a synonym for both of the other two words.

BANNER   (   )   DROOP

Answer: FLAG

6:   Underline the odd one out from 'questions'.

**QUESTIONS: QUIT, STONE, SCENT
TUNE, INSET, NOSE**

Answer: SCENT. There is no 'C' in 'questions'.

7:   Insert the missing number.

5	
6	

Answer: 30. Right = Top left x Bottom left.

8:   Insert the missing number:

4	5	3	3
6	8	7	2
5	15	4	

Answer: 5. Add column 1 to column 2, divide by column 3 for column 4. (5 + 15)/4 = 5.

9:   Insert the word that completes the first word and starts the second.

CL   (   )   ECT

Answer: ASP (Clasp and Aspect).

10:   Underline whether the final phrase is TRUE or FALSE.

All chairs are cheeses. All cheeses have three ears. Those with three ears grow on trees. All chairs grow on trees.

(TRUE)   (FALSE)

Answer: TRUE

11: Using the key, insert the sum of values surrounding each of the letters.

Key: £ = 1 @ = 2 & = 3

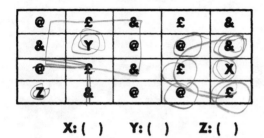

X: ( ) Y: ( ) Z: ( )

Answers: **X** = 3 + 2 + 1 + 2 + 1 = 9
 Y = 2 + 1 + 3 + 3 + 2 + 2 + 1 + 3 = 17
 Z = 2 + 1 + 3 = 6

12: Insert word prefixed by the letters on the left.

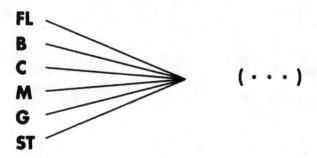

FL
B
C
M
G
ST

(• • •)

Answer: OAT

There are also questions giving suffixes and for a common prefix.

13:   Insert the number of the missing figure.

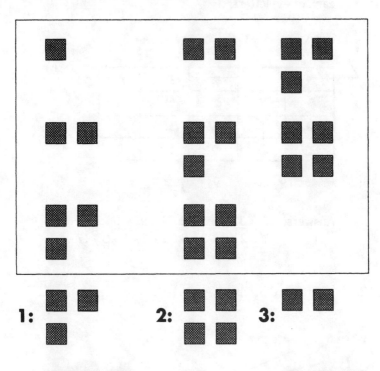

1:

2:

3:

4:

5:

6:

Answer: 6

14: Insert the missing number.

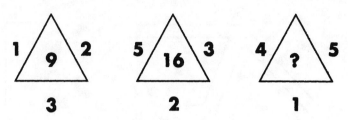

Answer: 9. Middle = Left + Right x Bottom.
Middle = (4 + 5) x 1 = 9.

15: Insert the missing number.

1   2   3   4   ____

Answer: 5. Add 1 to previous number.

16: There is a different design on each face of a six-sided cube. Underline whether the two cubes below are the SAME or DIFFERENT if rotated.

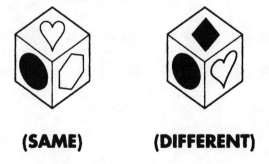

(SAME)   **(DIFFERENT)**

Answer: SAME

17: Insert the missing number.

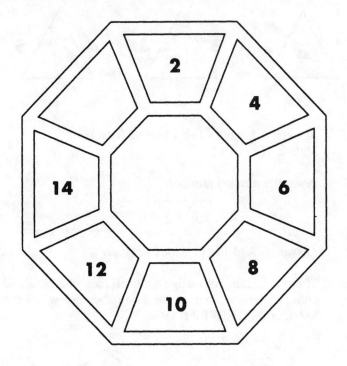

Answer: 16. Add 2 to previous number.

There are similar questions using letters.

18: Underline the odd one out.

ENO

WOT

EHRET

TCA

Answer: CAT. The others are numbers.

19:   What is this food?

ISFH   (_____)

Answer: FISH

Test 1

1: Insert the missing number.

16   22   28   34   (40)

2: Which of these is not a cheese?

DAME
CARDHDE
EARLECTV → sausage
GEERRUY

3: Insert the missing letter.

F   J   N   R   (V)

4: Insert the town from anagram.

ESTLETA   (Seattle)

5: Insert the missing numbers.

15 ⁺⁶ 21 ⁻³ 18 ⁺⁶ 24 ⁻³ (21) ⁺⁶ (27)

6: Insert the word which completes the first word and starts the second.

S (ℓ . . .) NT

7:   Select the correct figure from the six numbered ones.

1: **2:** **3:**

4: **5:** **6:**

8:   Insert the missing letters.

E   H   G   J   I   (K)   (H)

___

Test 1   61

9: Insert word prefixed by any of the letters on the left.

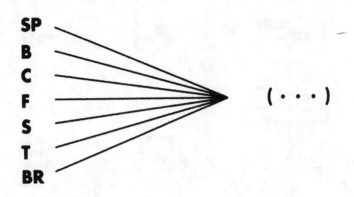

SP
B
C
F
S
T
BR

(. . .)

10: Insert the missing number.

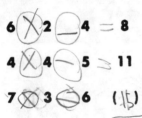

6 × 2 — 4 = 8

4 × 4 — 5 = 11

7 × 3 — 6 (⅓)

11: Underline whether the final phrase is TRUE or FALSE.

Some tractors are jugs; and most jugs have orange noses. All with orange noses quack; therefore some that quack are tractors.

(TRUE)   (FALSE)

12: Insert the missing number.

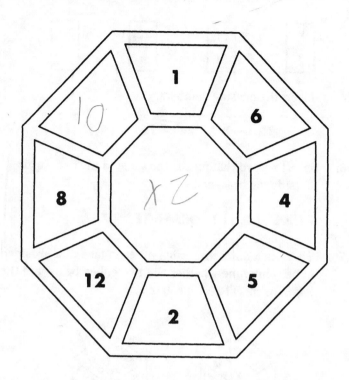

13: Insert word suffixed by any of the letters on the right.

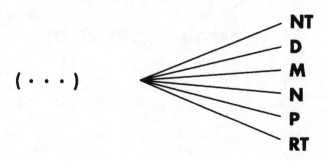

14: Insert the missing letters.

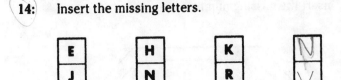

E
J

H
N

K
R

N
V

15: Insert the missing numbers.

4   12   8   24   16   (48)   (-)   (96)   (64)

32

16: Insert a word that means the same as the two words outside the brackets.

GUIDE (. . . .) GRAPHITE

17: There is a different design on each face of a six-sided cube. Underline whether the two cubes below are the SAME or DIFFERENT if rotated.

(SAME)   (DIFFERENT)

18: Select the correct figure from the six numbered ones.

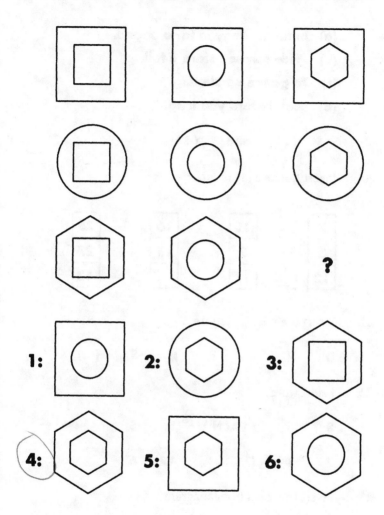

19: Which two phrases are the closest in meaning?

   (a) In for a penny in for a pound.
   (b) Pride comes before a fall.
   (c) To go the whole hog.
   (d) Look before you leap.

   (.)   and   (.)

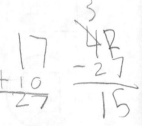

20: Insert the missing number.

7	+3	10	+6	16	+9	25
3	+4	7	+8	15	+12	27
12	+5	17	+10	27	+15	42

21: Insert the missing letters.

   D   V   F   T   H   R   (J)   (P)

22: Insert word.

   8   3   (EACH)   1   5

   7   1   (flag)   12   6

23: Insert the town from anagram.

   ALPNNASDIIOI   (I N D I A N A P O L I S)

24: Select the correct figure from the six numbered ones.

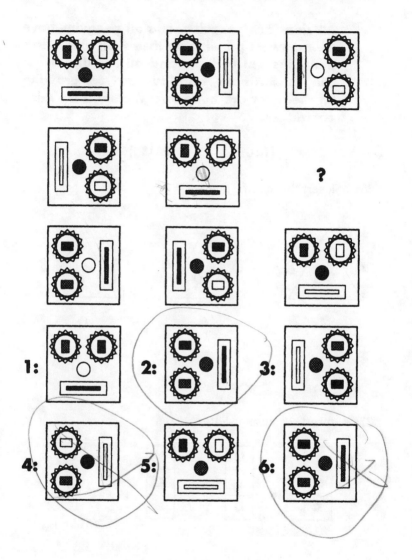

25: Underline whether the final phase is TRUE or FALSE.

All ships are penguins, and all penguins have lawnmowers growing on their feet; also, some penguins eat fridges; and all hairdriers eat fridges. But none with lawnmowers growing on their feet are hairdriers; therefore no ships eat fridges.

(TRUE) **(FALSE)**

26: Insert the missing number.

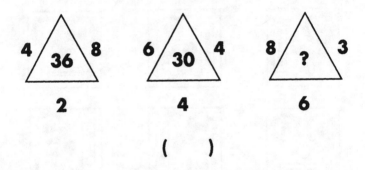

( )

27: Insert the missing letter.

J	M	G
O	S	K
S	U	

28: Insert the missing number.

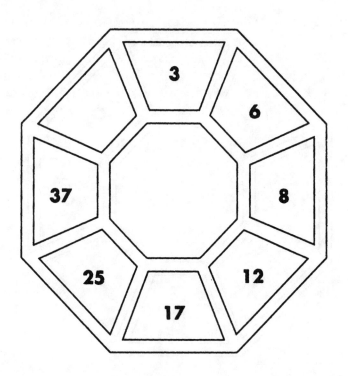

29: Underline the odd one out.

Psalms

Judges

Acts

Proverbs

30: Insert the missing letter.

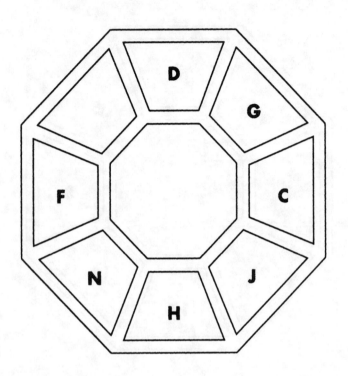

31: Insert the missing number.

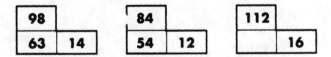

32: Insert the town from anagram.

DOTTIER (   )

33: Using the key below insert the sum of the values surrounding each of the letters.

Key: * = 4   ! = 5   & = 6

*	!	&	!	C
&	A	*	*	&
&	*	!	B	!
!	*	&	*	!

A: ( )   **B:** ( )   **C:** ( )

34: Insert the town from anagram.

GRIPHTUSTB   (   )

35: There is a different design on each face of a six-sided cube. Underline whether the two cubes below are the SAME or DIFFERENT if rotated.

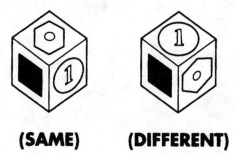

(SAME)   **(DIFFERENT)**

36: Select the correct figure from the six numbered ones.

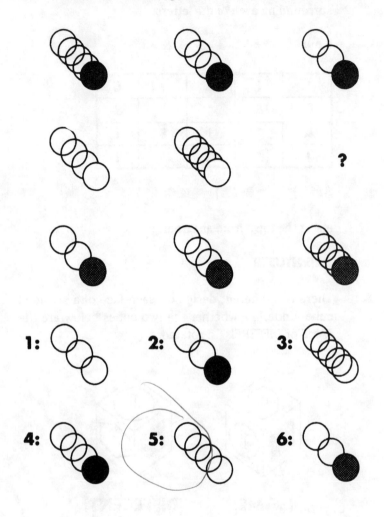

Test Your IQ

37: Insert the missing letter.

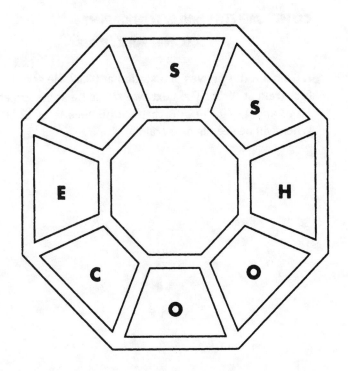

38: Which of these is not a boy's name?

NAAL

ROAMNN

RYSTEVELS

LPAIILRSC

39: Underline the odd one out from 'compliment'.

COMPLIMENT: MILE, TONIC, PINT
CLONE, MILK, PINE

40: A train spotter arrives at a station at 09.42. He sees his first train at 09.50. The next two trains he spots are at 10.40 and 11.40 The fourth train he sees is at 12.50. When will he see his next train?

Test 2

1: Insert the missing number.

45   41   37   33   (   )

2: Which of these is not a dog?

GROIC

EELABG

AORDBLAR

TTWEIHBAI

3: Insert the word which means the same as wrestle.

GR + (fruit) = (wrestle)

(   )

4: Insert the missing number.

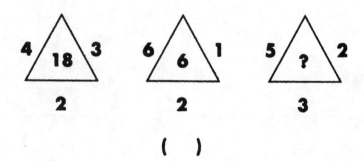

(   )

5: Select the correct figure from the six numbered ones.

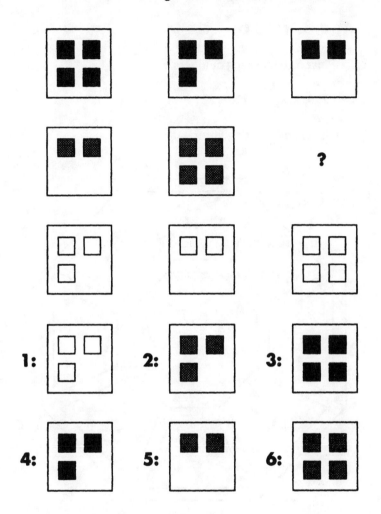

6:   Insert the missing letter.

   K   M   O   Q   ( )

7:   Insert the missing numbers.

   7   16   12   21   ( )   ( )

8:   Insert the missing letter.

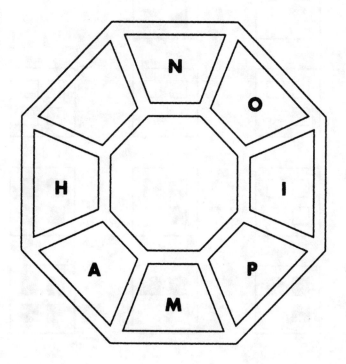

9: Insert the animal from anagram.

LEAF ( )

10: There is a different design on each face of a six-sided cube. Underline whether the two cubes below are the SAME or DIFFERENT if rotated.

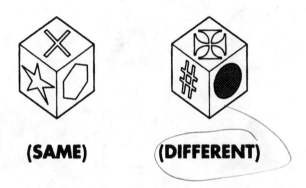

(SAME) **(DIFFERENT)**

11: Insert word prefixed by any of the letters on the left.

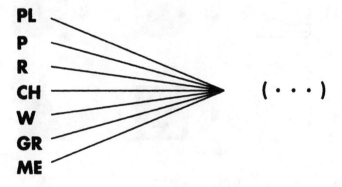

PL
P
R
CH
W
GR
ME

(∙ ∙ ∙)

12: Select the correct figure from the six numbered ones.

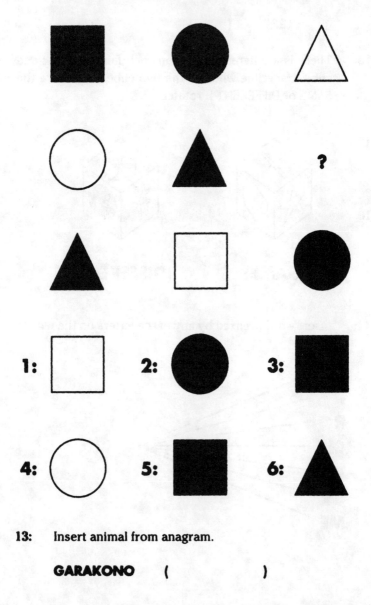

1: **2:** **3:**

4: **5:** **6:**

13: Insert animal from anagram.

GARAKONO   (   )

14: Underline whether the final phrase is TRUE or FALSE.

Some goblins are snowflakes; and several snowflakes are good at basketball; all that are good at basketball have three heads; therefore all that have three heads are goblins.

(TRUE) **(FALSE)**

15: Insert the missing letters.

V   W   U   V   T   ( )   ( )

16: Using the key below insert the sum of the values surrounding each of the letters.

Key: % = 2 (= 6 $ = 9

Q	(	(	(	$
$	%	%	P	%
(	R	$	%	(
%	$	(	$	(

P: (   ) **Q: (   )** **R: (   )**

17: Underline the odd one out from 'general'.

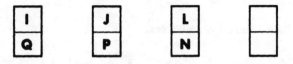

GENERAL: RAGE, GATE, EAGER
LARGE, LEAN, GALE

18: Insert the missing letters.

I		J		L		
Q		P		N		

19: Insert the missing number.

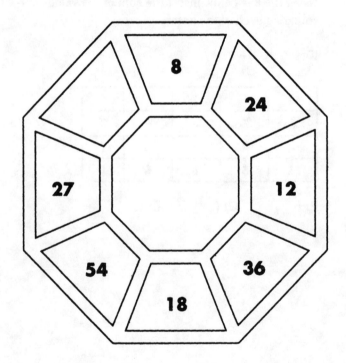

20: Insert the word that completes the first word and starts the second.

MI (. . .) **LE**

21: Insert the missing number.

15	
90	75

18	
108	90

21	
	105

22: Which of these is not a girl's name?

AILS

RIDING

SEAVSAN

PRODHANL

23: Insert word.

11   **3**   (**DUCK**)   **21**   **4**

20   **19**   (. . . .)   **15**   **16**

24: Insert animal from anagram.

SHRREGPAPSO   (   )

Select the correct figure from the six numbered ones.

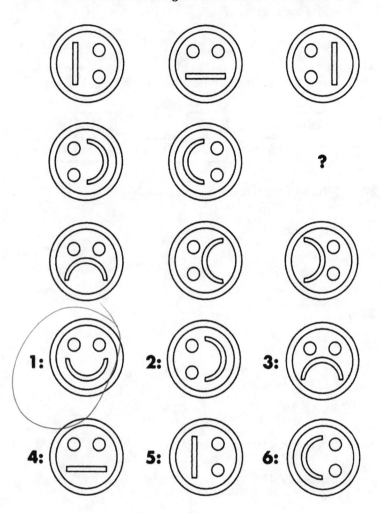

26:   Insert the missing numbers.

1   **3**   **4**   **12**   **16**   ( )   ( )

27:   There is a different design on each face of a six-sided
cube. Underline whether the two cubes below are the
SAME or DIFFERENT if rotated.

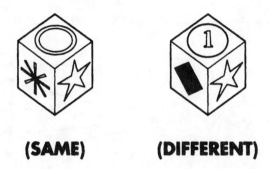

(SAME)   **(DIFFERENT)**

28:   Which two phrases are the closest in meaning?

(a)   **He who dares wins.**

(b)   **The end justifies the means.**

(c)   **Fortune favours the brave.**

(d)   **Stick to ones guns.**

(.)   **and**   (.)

29: Insert the missing number.

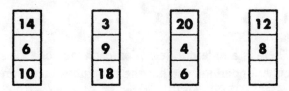

30: Insert word suffixed by any of the letters on the right.

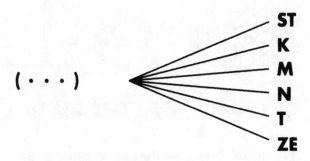

31: Underline the odd one out.

Lima

Berne

Sydney

Colombo

Budapest

32: Select the correct figure from the six numbered ones.

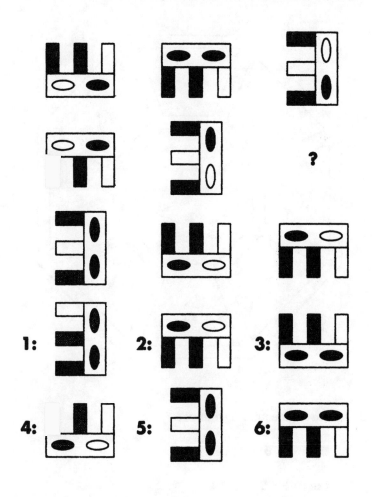

33: Insert the missing letters.

G   T   J   Q   M   N   ( )   ( )

34: Insert the missing letter.

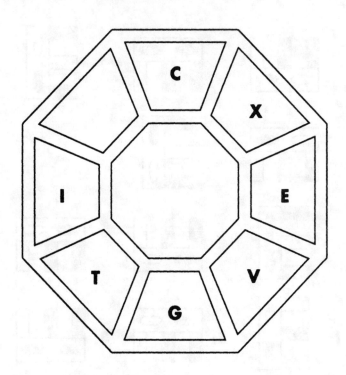

35: Insert the missing number.

14	6	4	5
8	40	24	2
9	18	3	( )

36: Insert the missing number.

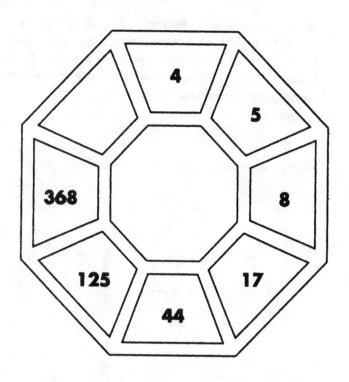

37: Insert animal from anagram.

RAGLATOIL (   )

38: Insert the missing letter.

39: Underline whether the final phrase is TRUE or FALSE.

All goats are sunglasses, and all sunglasses swim to work; also some sunglasses are made from grapes; and some chairs are made from grapes. But no chair swims to work; therefore some goats are made from grapes.

(TRUE)   (FALSE)

40: What three letters result from the following addition?

$$
\begin{array}{c}
\text{D B I} \\
\text{C D D} \\
\hline
(\,.\;.\;.\,) \\
\hline
\end{array}
$$

Test 3

1:   Insert the missing number.

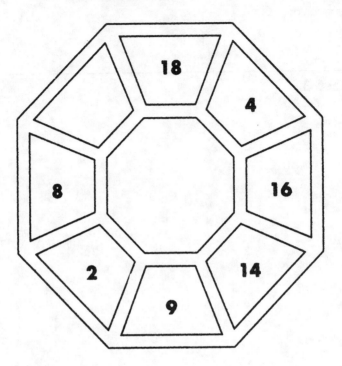

2:   Which of these is not a colour?

YNAC

TNEUTMAOG

ORNICMS

PRESAPIH

3:   Insert the tree from anagram.

LMPA   (   )

4: Select the correct figure from the six numbered ones.

1: **2:** **3:**

4: **5:** **6:**

5: Insert the missing number.

6 **9** **12** **15** (18)

Insert the missing letter.

C   H   M   R   ( )

7:    Using the key below insert the sum of the values surrounding each of the letters.

Key: % = 6   * = 7   @ = 8

W	*	%	*	@
@	%	*	F	%
*	*	@	*	%
@	B	%	@	*

B: ( )   F: ( )   W: ( )

8:    Insert word prefixed by any of the letters on the left.

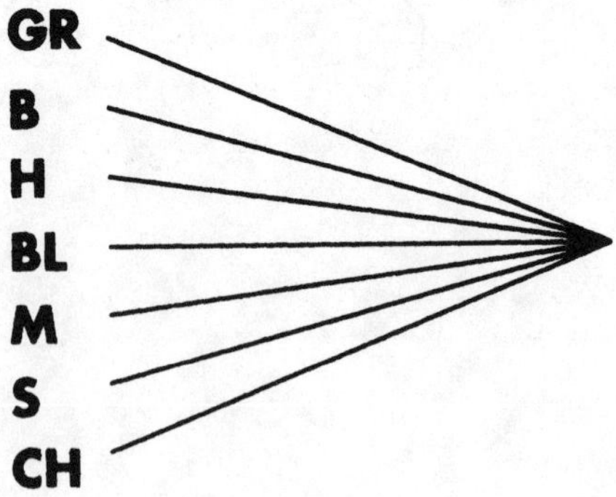

GR
B
H
BL
M
S
CH

(· · ·)

9: There is a different design on each face of a six-sided cube. Underline whether the two cubes below are the SAME or DIFFERENT if rotated.

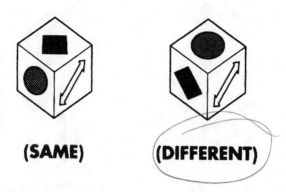

(SAME)   **(DIFFERENT)**

10: Insert the missing numbers.

34   26   32   24   ( )   ( )

11: Underline whether the final phrase is TRUE or FALSE.

Some tennis rackets are bankers; and all bankers have wings; all with wings drink pencil sharpeners; therefore all tennis rackets drink pencil sharpeners.

(TRUE)   (FALSE)

12: Insert the missing letter.

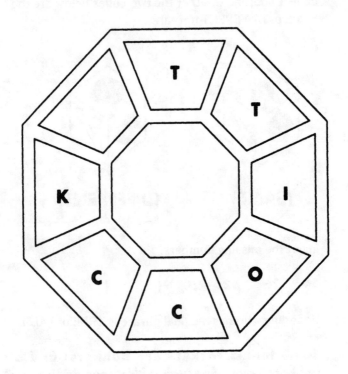

13: Insert the word that completes the first word and starts the second.

CON (. . . . .) **OR**

14: Insert the tree from anagram.

MPUL (PLUM)

15: Select the correct figure from the six numbered

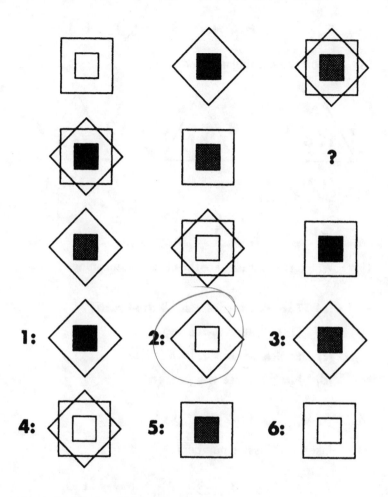

16: Insert the missing letters.

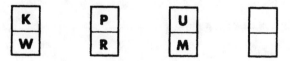

17: Insert the missing letters.

F   J   H   L   J   (N)   (L)

18: Insert the missing number.

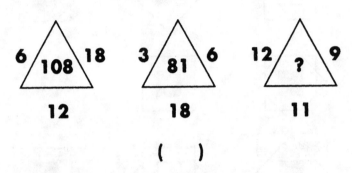

6 /108\ 18   3 /81\ 6   12 /?\ 9
12   18   11

( )

19: Which two phrases are the closest in meaning?

(a) **Too many cooks spoil the broth.**

(b) **Once bitten twice shy.**

(c) **Strike when the iron is hot.**

(d) **No time like the present.**

(.) and (.)

20: Insert the missing numbers.

2   8   6   24   18   (74)   (54)

21: Insert the tree from anagram.

CUTSPLYUAE   (24   )

22: Select the correct figure from the six numbered ones.

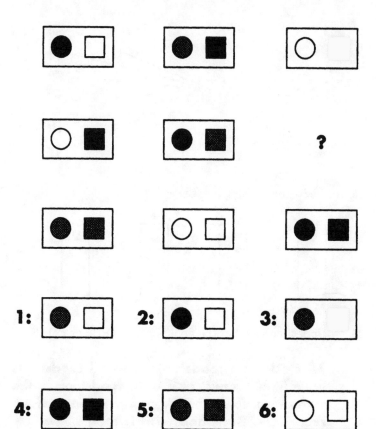

23: Insert the word which means the same as hankering.

Y + (deserving) = (hankering)

(   )

24: Insert word suffixed by any of the letters on the right.

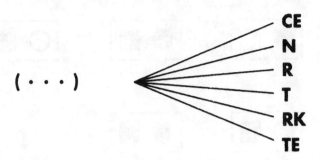

(· · ·)

CE
N
R
T
RK
TE

25: Insert the missing number.

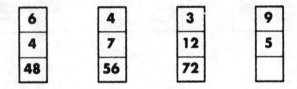

6
4
48

4
7
56

3
12
72

9
5

26: Underline whether the final phase is TRUE or FALSE.

All clocks are toadstools, and all toadstools have fifteen paws; also some toadstools make video recorders, and all crumpets make video recorders. But none with fifteen paws are crumpets; therefore no clocks make video recorders.

(TRUE)   (FALSE)

27: Insert the missing letters.

J   X   L   V   N   T   ( )   ( )

28: Insert word.

5   12   (FILE)   9   6

20   18   (....)   1   3

29: Insert the missing letter.

K		H		B
R		O		I
V		S		

30: Insert the missing number.

4	6	3	5
3	4	6	2
5	2	3	3
17	26	( )	13

31: Insert the tree from anagram.

MYROSCAE   (   )

32: Select the correct figure from the six numbered ones.

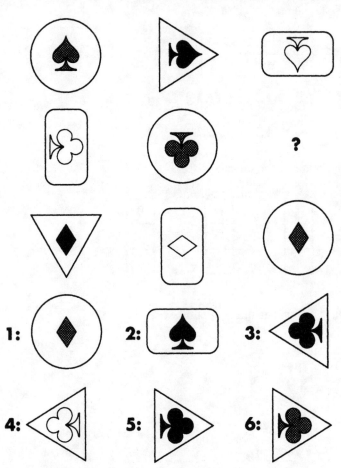

33: Underline the odd one out.

Horse

Bull

Lion

Ram

Goat

34: Insert the missing number.

96	
36	12

112	
42	14

48	
	6

35: Insert a word that means the same as the two words outside the brackets.

RESTAURANT (. . . . . . .) **FLASK**

36: Insert the missing number.

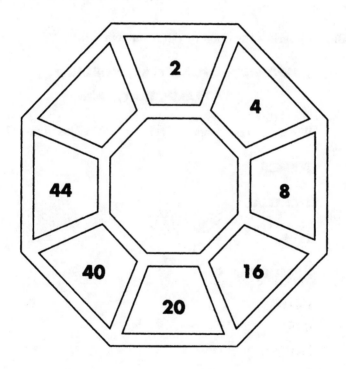

37: There is a different design on each face of a six-sided cube. Underline whether the two cubes below are the SAME or DIFFERENT if rotated.

 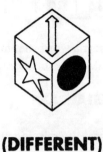

(SAME)   **(DIFFERENT)**

38: Underline the odd one out from 'temporary'.

TEMPORARY: **PORE, YEAR, MORTAR**
TRAMP, TRAY, CAMP

39: Which of these anagrams is not a musical instrument?

TEKLESR

TTCAENAS

TEUL

KPEENLSGOILC

40: Insert the missing letter.

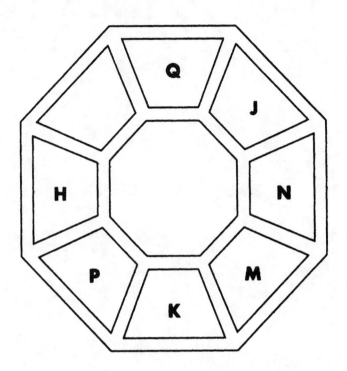

Test 4

1: Select the correct figure from the six numbered ones.

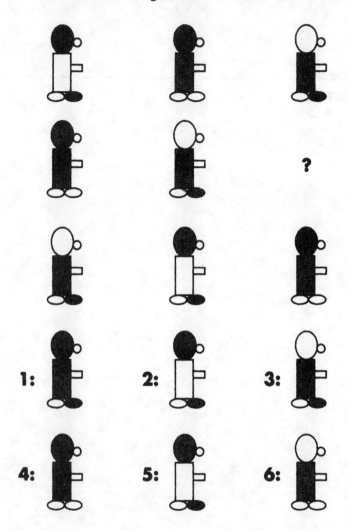

1: **2:** **3:**

4: **5:** **6:**

2: Insert the missing letter.

B   E   H   K   (N)

3: Underline whether the final phrase is TRUE or FALSE.

Some radiators are mice; and all mice can ride a bicycle. All who can ride a bicycle have floppy ears; therefore some radiators have floppy ears.

(TRUE) **(FALSE)**

4: Insert the missing letter.

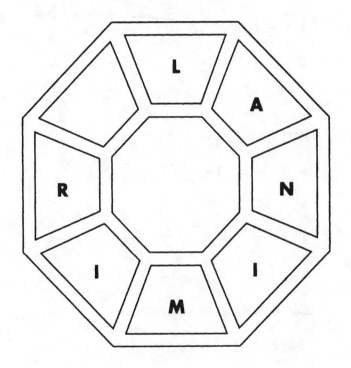

5: Insert the missing number.

55 50 45 40 (35)

6: Insert word suffixed by any of the letters on the right.

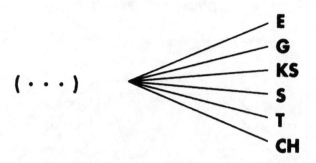

(...)

E
G
KS
S
T
CH

7: Insert the missing number.

19	14	16	32
4	8	2	4
3	3	2	7
5	2	( )	4

8: Insert the card game from anagram.

KORPE (Poker)

9: Insert the missing number.

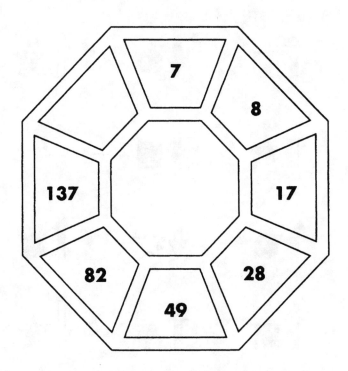

10: Insert the word that completes the first word and starts the second.

MU (. . . .) **LE**

11: Insert missing numbers.

9   7   12   10   (15)   (13)

12: Select the correct figure from the six numbered ones.

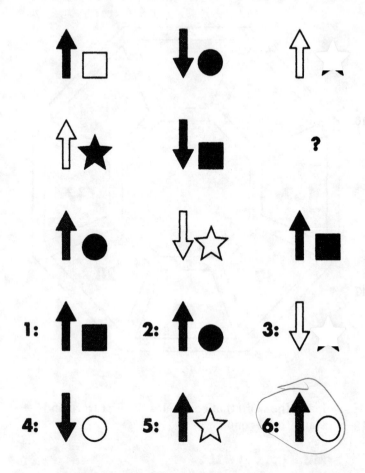

13: Insert a word that means the same as the two words outside the brackets.

ARRANGE (. . . . .) COMMAND

14: Insert the missing letters.

K   M   L   N   M   (*O*)   (*N*)

15: Insert the missing numbers.

2   6   8   24   32   (*96*)   (*128*)

16: Underline the odd one out.

Horn
Tusk
~~Purr~~
Fur
Paw

17: Insert the missing letter.

C		F		L
E		J		T
B		D		*H*

18: Insert card game from anagram.

ZUEBEIQ   (   )

19: There is a different design on each face of a six-sided cube. Underline whether the two cubes below are the SAME or DIFFERENT if rotated.

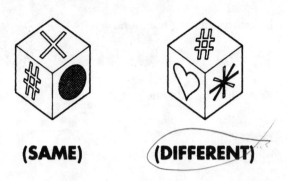

(SAME)   **(DIFFERENT)**

20: Insert the missing number.

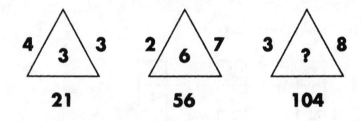

4   3   3   2   6   7   3   ?   8

21   56   104

21: Which of these is not a dance?

VEJI   **ANINMOCN**

DGAAFONN   **TNRCEAOSHL**

22: Insert the missing letters.

C   U   F   S   I   Q   (L)   (O)

23:   Select the correct figure from the six numbered ones.

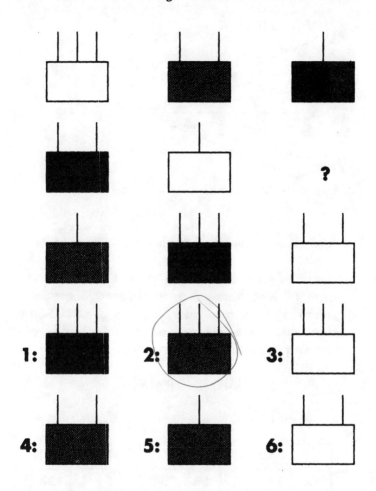

24:   Insert the card game from the anagram.

AANTSAC   (   )

25: Insert word prefixed by any of the letters on the left.

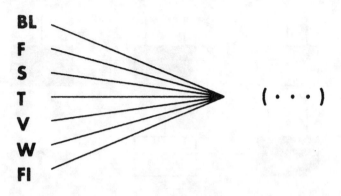

26: Underline whether the final phrase is TRUE or FALSE.

Some tulips are sausages, and all ghosts snore; also all telephones fear bookcases. Some telephones snore and all tulips are ghosts. Some bookcases are ghosts and all telephones are sausages, so all sausages snore.

(TRUE)   (FALSE)

27: Insert the missing number.

36	
72	108

28	
56	84

41	
	123

28: Using the key below insert the sum of the values surrounding each of the letters.

Key: ? = 8   # = 3 $ = 5

?	$	#	#	$
W	$	E	$	?
?	#	?	?	#
#	?	$	$	G

W: ( )   G: ( )   E: ( )

29: Which two phrases are the closest in meaning?

(a) Practise what you preach.

(b) Let sleeping dogs lie.

(c) Least said soonest mended.

(d) The exception proves the rule.

(.) and (.)

30: Insert the missing number.

15
13
20

12
10
18

16
18
12

11
13

31: Select the correct figure from the six numbered ones.

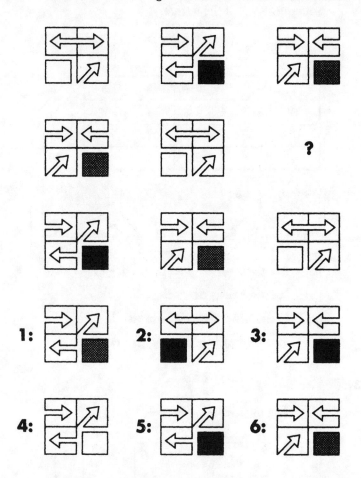

32: Underline the odd one out from 'devilish'.

DEVILISH: **HIVE, DISH, LIVID**
SHED, CIVIL, SIDE

33: Insert the missing number.

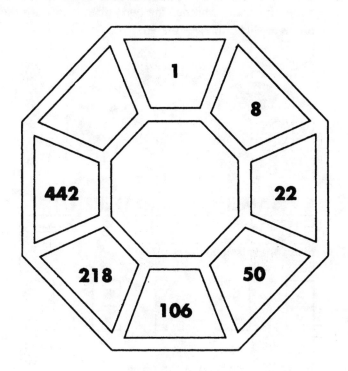

34: Insert word.

| 14 | 9 | (CHIN) | 8 | 3 |
| 16 | 19 | (. . . .) | 1 | 23 |

35: Insert the card game from anagram.

EETNICAP ( )

36: There is a different design on each face of a six-sided cube. Underline whether the two cubes below are the SAME or DIFFERENT if rotated.

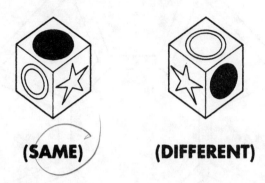

(SAME)   **(DIFFERENT)**

37: Insert the missing letters.

38: Which of these is not a composer?

Large

Bhestucr

Yvrisstakn

Kupcnihm

39: Insert the missing letter.

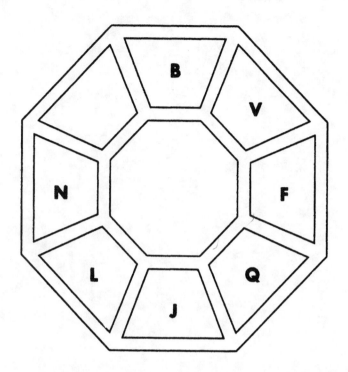

40: An ice-cream seller has six different varieties of ice-cream. If he sells two ice-creams at a time and the two flavours are always different, how many different combinations of flavours can he make?

Test 5

1: Underline the odd one out.

Carrot

Kohlrabi

Peach

Spinach

Mangetout

2: Using the key below insert the sum of the values surrounding each of the letters.

Key: ! = 4   @ = 6   { = 8

L	@	@	{	@
{	!	!	{	K
!	J	{	@	!
@	{	@	{	@

J: (   )   **K:** (   )   **L:** (   )

3: Insert the missing number.

9   14   19   24   (   )

4: Insert a word that means the same as the two words outside the brackets.

FRAMEWORK (. . . . . . .) **RASPING**

5: Insert the missing letter.

A   **E**   **I**   **M**   ( )

6: Insert the ship from anagram.

TOBA   ( )

7: Which two phrases are the closest in meaning?

(a) Cook the books.
(b) Make a meal of.
(c) Make a mountain of a mole hill.
(d) Take the rough with the smooth.

(.) and (.)

8: Insert word.

5   **4**   (RUDE)   **21**   **18**

5   **26**   (. . . .)   **1**   **13**

9: Select the correct figure from the six numbered ones.

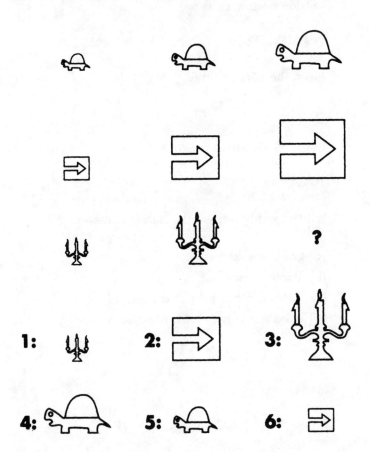

1:

2:

3:

4:

5:

6:

10: Insert the word that completes the first word and starts the second.

C (. . . .) O

11: Insert the missing numbers.

4   8   6   10   ( )   ( )

12: Insert the missing letters.

L   O   N   Q   P   ( )   ( )

13: Underline whether the final phrase is TRUE or FALSE.

All boxes are guitars; and all guitars are good wrestlers. Some good wrestlers have webbed feet; so some boxes have webbed feet.

(TRUE)   (FALSE)

14: Insert the missing number.

14		10		15		9
19		15		20		14
86		82		87		

15: Insert the ship from anagram.

RATEEMS   (   )

16: Insert the missing number.

4	9	15	6
8	6	5	15
2	3	( )	24

17: There is a different design on each face of a six-sided cube. Underline whether the two cubes below are the SAME or DIFFERENT if rotated.

(SAME)   **(DIFFERENT)**

18: Which of these is not a bird?

KARL   BGANRYREOL

GUNPINE   EAGIUGRBRD

19: Insert the missing numbers.

3   9   6   18   12   ( )   ( )

20: Select the correct figure from the six numbered ones.

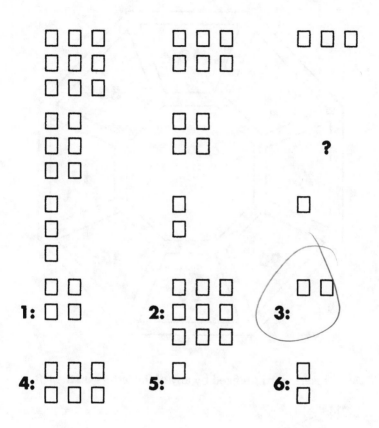

21: Insert the missing number.

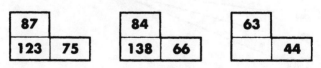

22: Insert the missing number.

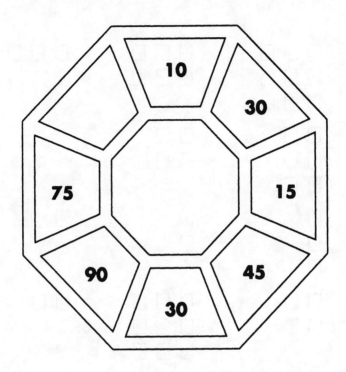

23: Insert word prefixed by any of the letters on the left.

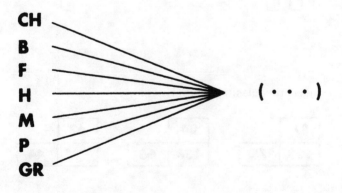

24: Insert the missing letter.

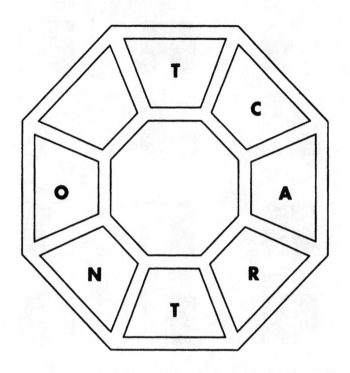

25: Insert word suffixed by any of the letters on the right.

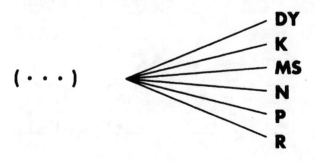

26: Select the correct figure from the six numbered ones.

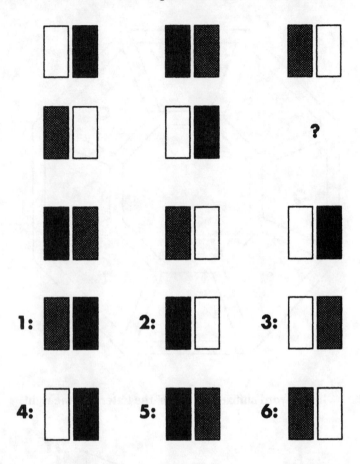

27: Insert the missing letters.

X		T		P		
A		D		G		

28: Insert the missing letters.

P   T   Q   Q   R   N   (⅃)   ( )

29: Underline whether the final phrase is TRUE or FALSE.

All socks are frogs and all frogs have four beaks; also some lights can cook and all that can cook have four beaks, and some frogs squeak. All socks are lights, therefore some lights squeak.

(TRUE)   (FALSE)

30: There is a different design on each face of a six-sided cube. Underline whether the two cubes below are the SAME or DIFFERENT if rotated.

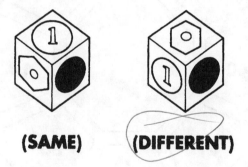

(SAME)   (DIFFERENT)

31: Insert the ship from anagram.

RURCISE ( )

32: Underline the odd one out from 'rectangle'.

RECTANGLE: **REAL, TINGE, CRATE**
GRATE, LARGE, RANG

33: Insert the missing number.

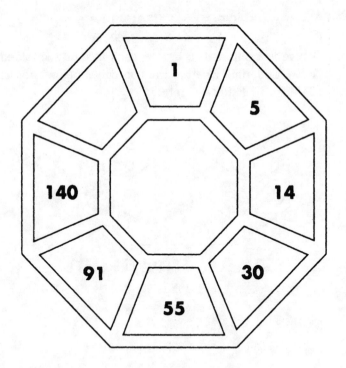

34: Insert the ship from anagram.

PTEBSTILAH   (   )

35: Insert the missing letter.

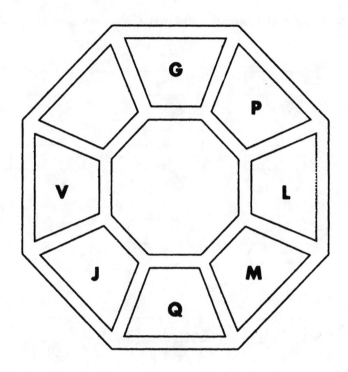

36: Which of these is not a vegetable?

NABE   **TOTOPA**

TGOETUCRE   **HEENVOBTE**

37: In a quiz, Alan partners Bess, Colin partners Debbie and Eric partners Fran. Who partners Greg?

PETER   **HARRY**   **TONY**   **PHILLIP**

38: Select the correct figure from the six numbered ones.

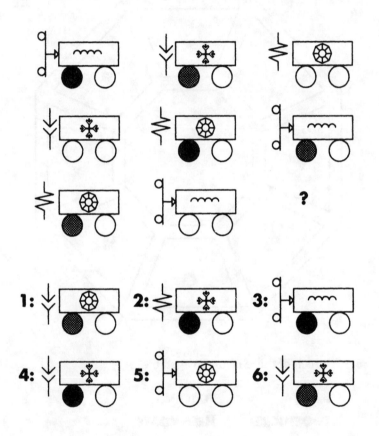

39: Insert the missing letter.

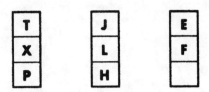

40: Insert the missing number.

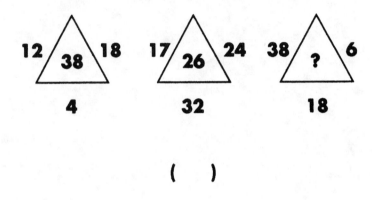

( )

Test 6

1:     Insert the missing number.

36   30   24   18   ( )

2:     Which of these is not an item of furniture?

HIRAC
ATRIGU
BPACOUDR
SEDRESR

3:     Insert the missing letter.

D   G   J   M   ( )

4:     Insert the shape from anagram.

CRILEC   (   )

5:     Insert the missing numbers.

20   40   30   50   ( )   ( )

6:     Insert the word which completes the first word and starts the second.

EN   (. . . .)   RSE

7:   Select the correct figure from the six numbered ones.

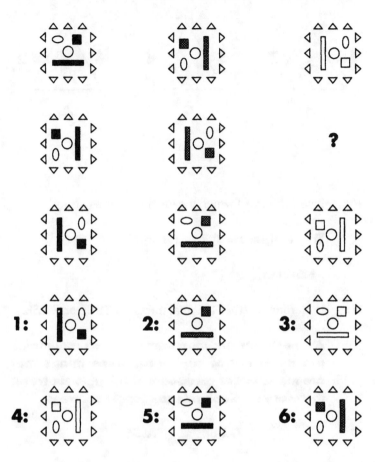

8:   Insert missing letters.

N   P   O   Q   P   ( )   ( )

9: Insert the missing number.

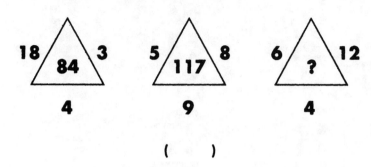

18 / 84 / 3
4

5 / 117 / 8
9

6 / ? / 12
4

( )

10: Insert the word which means the same as strand.

TH + (perused) = (strand)

ANSWER: ( )

11: Underline whether the final phrase is TRUE or FALSE.

All elephants are mountains; and all mountains are made out of cupboard. Some things that are made out of cardboard can juggle six trees; therefore all elephants can juggle six trees.

(TRUE)   (FALSE)

12: Insert the shape from anagram.

NHEADTOTERR   (   )

13: Insert the missing number.

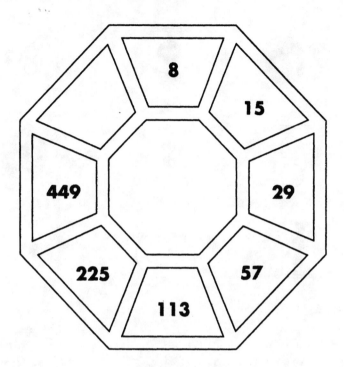

8

15

449

29

225

57

113

14: Insert word.

11   19   (**MASK**)   1   13

20   9   (. . . .)   24   5

15: Insert the missing letters.

I   J   L   I   O   H   ( )   ( )

16: Select the correct figure from the six numbered ones.

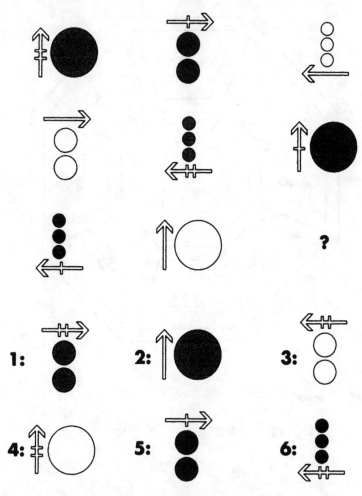

17: Underline the odd one out from 'alarming'.

ALARMING: **MAIN, GRAIL, TRAIL**
RING, NAIL, GRAIN

18:   Insert the missing letter.

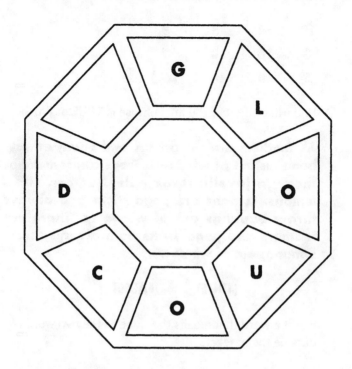

19:   Which of these is not an English town or city ?

GORHINBT   **CRETESHAMN**

AFDORSTTR   **TTMEODRRA**

20:   Insert the missing numbers.

3   6   9   18   27   ( )   ( )

21: Insert the missing number.

10	4	5	9
3	13	10	5
8	4	6	( )

22: Underline whether the final phrase is TRUE or FALSE.

All feathers are car drivers and always throw bananas out of windows. Frogs can sometimes throw a javelin three miles, as can some lemons. Lemons are pogo sticks and always throw bananas out of windows. Therefore feathers and pogo sticks both always throw bananas out of windows.

(TRUE)   (FALSE)

23: Insert a word that means the same as the two words outside the brackets.

DECORATIVE   (. . . . .)   WHIM

24: There is a different design on each face of a six-sided cube. Underline whether the two cubes below are the SAME or DIFFERENT if rotated.

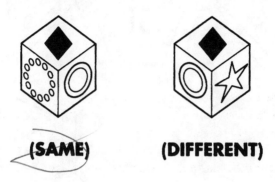

(SAME)   **(DIFFERENT)**

25: Underline the odd one out.

Sovereign

Crown

Florin

Shilling

Sixpence

26: Insert the missing letters.

J		L		N		
M		J		G		

27: Insert the missing number.

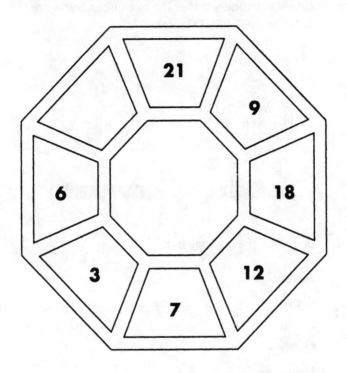

28: Insert word prefixed by any of the letters on the left.

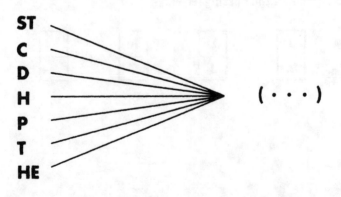

29: Select the correct figure from the six numbered ones.

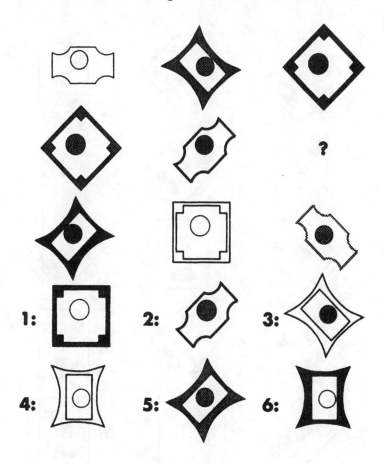

1: **2:** **3:**

4: **5:** **6:**

30: Insert the missing number.

3		
30		
18		

10		
37		
25		

2		
29		
17		

14		
41		

31: Select the correct figure from the six numbered ones.

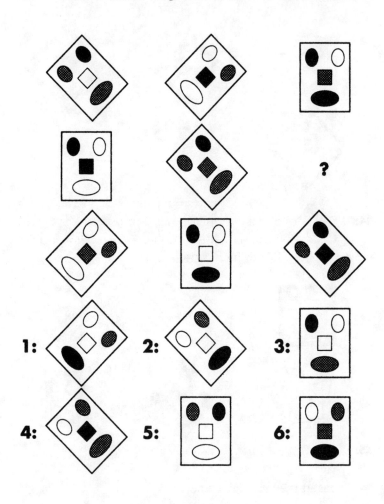

32: Insert the missing number.

9	
3	12

15	
11	17

37	
	45

33: Using the key below insert the sum of the values surrounding each of the letters.

Key:) = 3   % = 7 $ = 5

%	%	$	)	T
)	Z	)	%	$
)	%	$	W	%
%	$	)	$	)

T: ( )   **W:** ( )   **Z:** ( )

34: There is a different design on each face of a six-sided cube. Underline whether the two cubes below are the SAME or DIFFERENT if rotated.

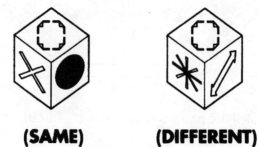

(SAME)   **(DIFFERENT)**

35: Insert the shape from anagram.

CEEGNRALT   (   )

36: Insert the missing letter.

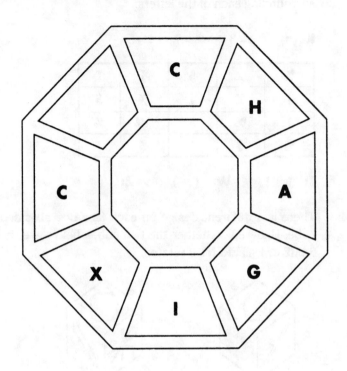

37: Which two phrases are the closest in meaning?

(a) **To the victor the spoils.**

(b) **Every picture tells a story.**

(c) **Time and tide wait for no man.**

(d) **The champion wins the trophy.**

(.) **and** (.)

38: Insert word suffixed by any of the letters on the right.

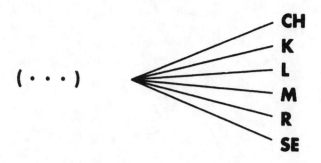

(. . .)

CH
K
L
M
R
SE

39: Insert the missing letter.

M
O
Q

T
V
X

F
H

40: Insert the shape from anagram.

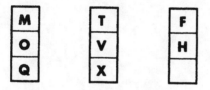

ARGINELT   (   )

Test 7

1: Select the correct figure from the six numbered ones.

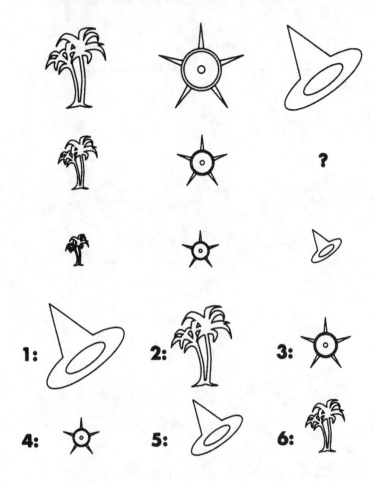

1:   **2:**   **3:**

4:   **5:**   **6:**

2: Which of these is not a fish?

LECIPA

SLUTOC

AIRENSD

CLAREMEK

3: Insert the missing number.

7   15   23   31   (   )

4: Insert the missing number.

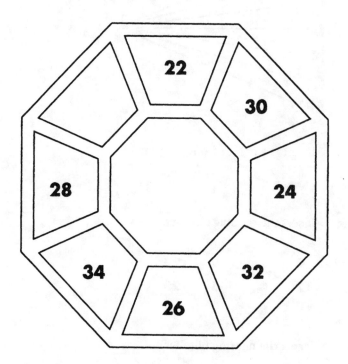

5: Insert a word that means the same as the two words outside the brackets.

FOLLOW   (. . . . .)   STEM

6: Insert word prefixed by any of the letters on the left.

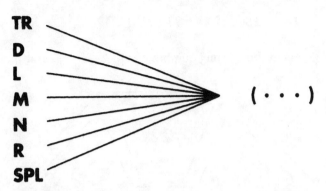

TR
D
L
M
N
R
SPL

(· · ·)

7: Insert the colour from anagram.

ENGER   (   )

8: Insert the missing number.

9	2	5	29
12	4	3	26
15	8	( )	15

9: Insert the missing number.

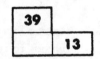

42	
7	21

46	
6	18

39	
	13

10: Insert the missing letter.

H   J   L   N   ( )

11: Select the correct figure from the six numbered ones.

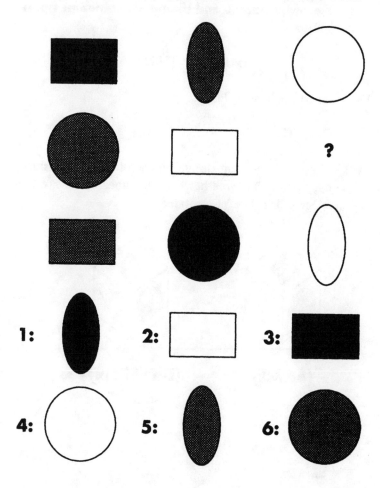

12: Underline whether the final phrase is TRUE or FALSE.

All cornflakes are horses. All cornflakes have red buttons and sometimes play bingo. Scones sometimes play bingo. Diamonds are scones, therefore horses and diamonds sometimes play bingo.

(TRUE)   (FALSE)

13: Insert the missing letters.

C   G   E   I   G   ( )   ( )

14: There is a different design on each face of a six-sided cube. Underline whether the two cubes below are the SAME or DIFFERENT if rotated.

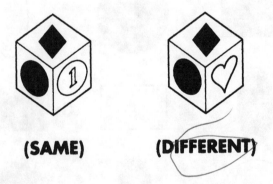

(SAME)   (DIFFERENT)

15: Insert colour from anagram.

GAMATEN ( )

16: Insert the missing letter.

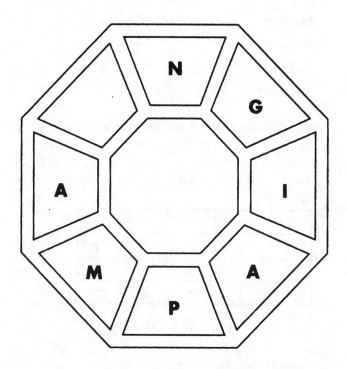

17: Insert the word that completes the first word and starts the second.

CONTR (. . .) **IVE**

18: Insert the missing numbers.

25   15   18   8   ( )   ( )

19: Underline the odd one out.

Mozart

Wagner

Haydn

Schubert

20: Using the key below insert the sum of the values surrounding each of the letters.

Key: @ = 5   ! = 6   * = 7

W	*	*	*	*
!	@	Y	@	!
@	*	!	!	X
*	!	*	@	*

W: (   )   X: (   )   Y: (   )

21: Insert the missing letters.

G
S

J
P

P
J

22: Insert the correct figure from the six numbered ones.

23: Insert the missing numbers.

2   4   6   12   18   ( )   ( )

24: Insert the missing letters.

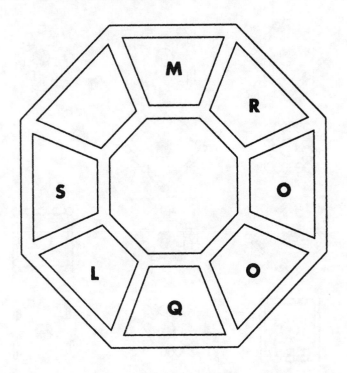

25: Insert word suffixed by any of the letters on the right.

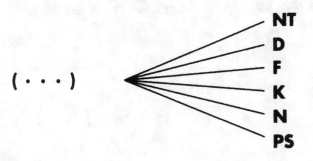

$(\cdot \cdot \cdot)$

NT
D
F
K
N
PS

Test Your IQ

26: Which two phrases are the closest in meaning?

    (a)   **Is the tide turning?**

    (b)   **Are you lost for words?**

    (c)   **Can an early bird get the worm?**

    (d)   **Has the cat got your tongue?**

                   (.)   **and**   **(.)**

27: Insert colour from anagram.

    ENTRAGENI   **(**   **)**

28: Insert the missing number.

8		16		32		64
4		12		36		108
2		8		32		

29: Underline the odd one out from 'complicate'.

    COMPLICATE: **TIMER, PLATE, MAIL**

                           COAT, CLIP, TAME

30: Insert word.

    20   **15**   **(PLOT)**   **12**   **16**

    5   **7**   **(. . . .)**   **18**   **21**

31: Select the correct figure from the six numbered ones.

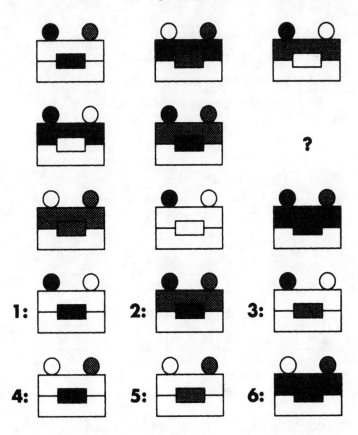

32: Which of these is not a planet?

PREJITU   **NATRUS**
TUPOL   **SUGATU**

33: Insert the missing number.

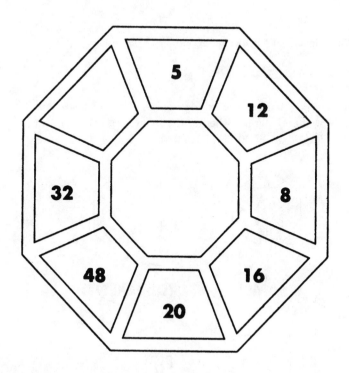

34: Insert the missing number.

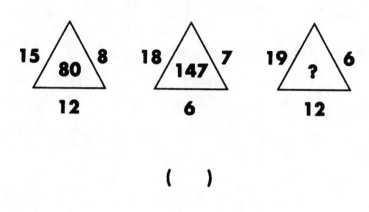

( )

35: Insert colour from anagram.

USTUIOREQ (　　　　　)

36: There is a different design on each face of a six-sided cube. Underline whether the two cubes below are the SAME or DIFFERENT if rotated.

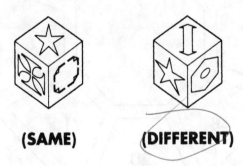

(SAME) **(DIFFERENT)**

37: Insert the missing letter.

F
I
M

L
O
S

Q
T

38: Insert the word which means the same as sill.

L + (border) = (sill)

(　　　　)

39: Insert the missing letters.

V   J   W   H   X   F   ( )   ( )

40: Underline whether the final phrase is TRUE or FALSE.

Some postcards are polar bears, and some washing machines sneeze a lot; also hedgehogs speak Chinese, and all that speak Chinese sneeze a lot. But no polar bears sneeze a lot. Some washing machines speak Chinese and all postcards are washing machines. Therefore some postcards speak Chinese.

(TRUE)   (FALSE)

Test 8

1: Insert the missing number.

34   27   20   13   ( )

2: Which of these is not a drink?

INCHKEC
GANCOC
ULTIAQE
NEMACAPHG

3: Insert the missing letter.

B   G   L   Q   ( )

4: Insert the tool from anagram.

ENKIF   (   )

5: Insert the missing numbers.

40   33   37   30   ( )   ( )

6: Insert the word which completes the first word and starts the second.

ASTE (. . . .) Y

7: Select the correct figure from the six numbered ones.

  ?

1:   **2:**   **3:**

4:   **5:**   **6:**

8: Insert the missing letters.

K	L	J	M	
R	Q	S	P	

9: Insert word prefixed by any of the letters on the left.

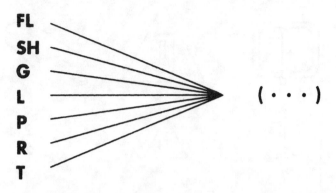

FL
SH
G
L
P
R
T

(· · ·)

10: Insert a word that means the same as the two words outside the brackets.

GLASS   (. . . . . . .)   ACROBAT

11: Underline whether the final phrase is TRUE or FALSE.

All skates are pegs. Pegs sometimes write poems and igloos sometimes paint masks. Cups paint masks and are dolphins. Dolphins never write poems, so skates and cups can both write poems.

(TRUE)   (FALSE)

12: Insert the missing number.

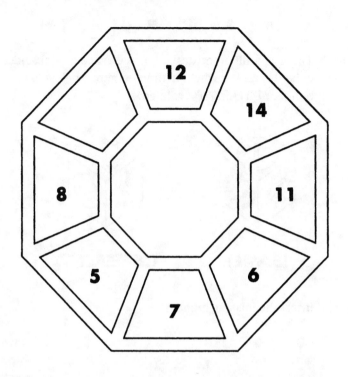

13: Insert word suffixed by any of the letters on the right.

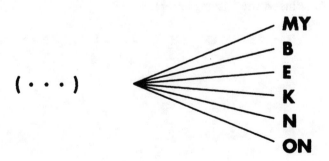

14: Insert the missing numbers.

1   4   3   12   9   ( )   ( )

15: There is a different design on each face of a six-sided cube. Underline whether the two cubes below are the SAME or DIFFERENT if rotated.

(SAME)   **(DIFFERENT)**

16: Insert the missing number.

18	6	14	3
12	3	7	2
6	27	15	( )

17: Insert the missing letters.

R   S   Q   R   P   ( )   ( )

18: Select the correct figure from the six numbered ones.

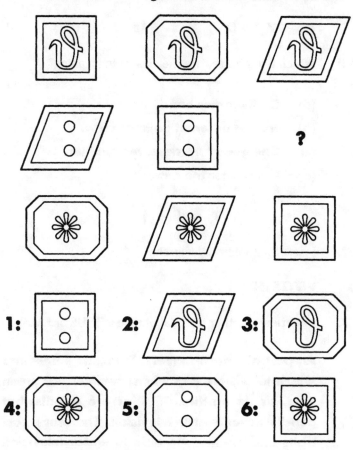

1: **2:** **3:**

4: **5:** **6:**

19: Insert the missing number.

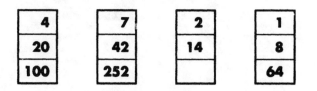

4	7	2	1
20	42	14	8
100	252		64

20: Insert the missing letters.

B   Z   D   Y   F   X   ( )   ( )

21: Which two phrases are the closest in meaning?

(a)   **On the other hand.**

(b)   **From a different point of view.**

(c)   **One good turn deserves another.**

(d)   **The sooner the better.**

(.)   and   (.)

22: Insert the tool from anagram.

WETZEESR   (   )

23: Underline whether the final phrase is TRUE or FALSE.

All portraits are trumpets. Trumpets sometimes watch television. Portraits sometimes eat green hats, as do muffins. Muffins are pencils, but pencils never watch television. Therefore portraits and muffins are able to watch television together.

(TRUE)   (FALSE)

24: Select the correct figure from the six numbered ones.

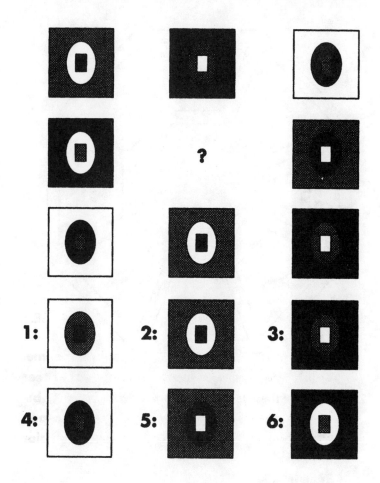

25: Insert the missing number.

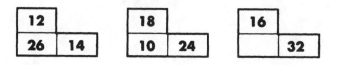

26: Insert the missing number.

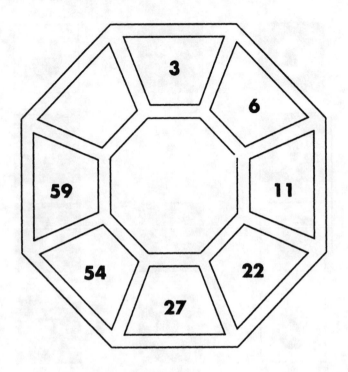

27: Which of these is not a sport?

LOFG

TRECCKI

BRENIMASU

HASSQU

28: Insert the missing letter.

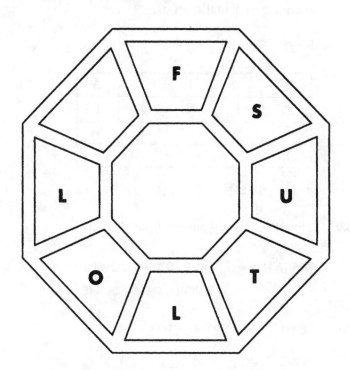

29: Insert the tool from anagram.

IWRDSEEVCRR (   )

30: Insert word.

| 16 | 9 | (QUIP) | 21 | 17 |
| 20 | 19 | (. . . .) | 5 | 22 |

31: Using the key below insert the sum of the values surrounding each of the letters.

Key: $ = 7   % = 6   ! = 5

$	%	!	!	$
%	!	K	%	!
$	%	$	$	M
L	!	!	%	$

K: (   )   L: (   )   M: (   )

32: Underline the odd one out from 'deviation'.

DEVIATION: DIVE, TOAD, VOICE

AVOID, INTO, DONE

33: Insert the tool from anagram.

WACASHK   (   )

34: Insert the word that means the same as disgrace.

DE + (rank) = (disgrace)

(   )

35: Select the correct figure from the six numbered ones.

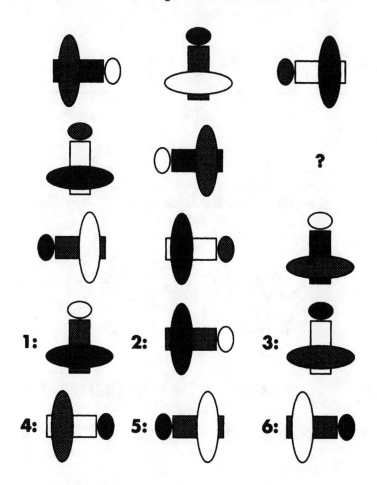

1: **2:** **3:**

4: **5:** **6:**

36: Insert the missing letter.

W		Q		I
T		N		F
R		L		

37: Insert the missing number.

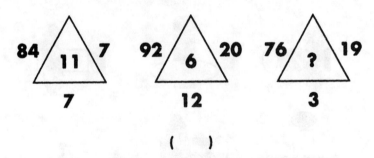

( )

38: There is a different design on each face of a six-sided cube. Underline whether the two cubes below are the SAME or DIFFERENT if rotated.

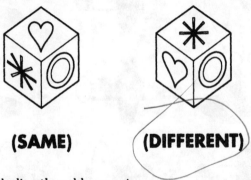

(SAME) **(DIFFERENT)**

39: Underline the odd one out.

January
May
June
August
December

40: Insert the missing letter.

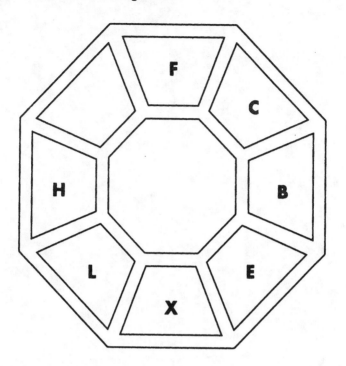

Part Three: Answers

1:      **40**. Add 6 to previous number.

2:      **EARLECTV**. Cervelat is a sausage.
        Edam, Cheddar, Gruyere are cheeses.

3:      **V**. Add 4 to previous letter.

4:      **SEATTLE**

5:      **21, 27**. Alternately add 6 and subtract 3
        i. e. 24 - 3 = 21 + 6 = 27.

6:      **PARE, PATE and TALE** are all valid answers.

7:      **6**

8:      **L, K**. Add 2 to each letter to get the next-but-one letter
        along i.e. J + 2 = L and I + 2 = K.

9:      **OIL**

10:     **15**. Multiply first column by second, and then
        subtract the third i.e. (7 x 3) - 6 = 15.

11:     **TRUE**

12: **10**. Opposites are doubles.

13: **SKI**

14: **N, V**. Top row add 3 and bottom row add 4
i.e. K + 3 = N and R + 4 = V.

15: **48, 32**. Alternately multiply by 3 and subtract
the previous number i.e. 16 x 3 = 48 - 16 = 32.

16: **LEAD**

17: **SAME**

18: **4**

19: **a and c**

20: **27**. First row add 3, 6, 9, second add 4, 8, 12
and third add 5, 10, 15 i.e. 17 + 10 = 27.

21: **J, P**. Alternately add 2 and subtract 2
i.e. H + 2 = J and R - 2 = P.

22: **FLAG**

23: **INDIANAPOLIS**

24: **2**

25: **FALSE**. Some ships eat fridges.

26: **32**. Multiply left number by right number, add bottom
number and add 2 to give the middle number
i.e. (8 x 3) + 6 + 2 = 32.

27: **Q.** Multiply by 2 the difference between first and second column, then subtract from second column to get the third i.e. U - (2 x 2) = Q.

28: **56.** Add each number to the previous one, then subtract 1, 2, 3 etc. i.e. 37 + 25 - 6 = 56.

29: **ACTS.** Acts is from the New Testament. The others are from the Old Testament.

30: **T.** Opposites are doubles.

31: **72.** Bottom left number is half top number added to bottom right number i.e. (112 / 2) + 16 = 72.

32: **DETROIT**

33: **A = 40 B = 39 C = 15**

34: **PITTSBURGH**

35: **DIFFERENT**

36: **1**

37: **K.** Alternate words spell SHOE and SOCK.

38: **LPAIILRSC.** Priscilla is a girl's name. Alan, Norman and Sylvester are boys' names.

39: **MILK.** There is no 'K' in 'compliment'.

40: **14.10 (or 2.10 p.m.).** Time increases 10 minutes i.e. 12.50 + 80 minutes = 14.10.

Test 2 Answers

1: **29**. Subtract 4 from previous number.

2: **TTWEIHBAI**. Whitebait is a fish.
Corgi, Beagle and Labrador are dogs.

3: **GRAPPLE**

4: **24**. Multiply numbers outside, then subtract 6 for
middle number i.e. (5 x 2 x 3) - 6 = 24.

5: **2**

6: **S**. Add 2 to previous letter.

7: **17, 26**. Alternately add 9 and subtract 4
i.e. 21 - 4 = 17 + 9 = 26.

8: **C**. Sequence spells 'champion' backwards.

9: **FLEA**

10: **SAME**

11: **ANT**

12: **3**

13: **KANGAROO**

14: **TRUE**

15: **U, S**. Alternately add 1 and subtract 2
i.e. T + 1 = U - 2 = S.

16: **P = 42   Q = 17   R = 45**

17: **GATE**. There is no 'T' in 'general'.

18: **O, K**
Top row add 1, 2, 3 etc. and bottom row subtract 1, 2,
3 etc. i.e. L + 3 = O and N - 3 = K.

19: **81**. Alternately multiply by 3 and divide by 2
i.e. 27 x 3 = 81.

20: **STY**

21: **126**. Bottom left number is bottom right number plus
top number i.e. 105 + 21 = 126.

22: **PRODHANL**. Randolph is a boy's name.
Lisa, Ingrid and Vanessa are girls' names.

23: **POST**

24: **GRASSHOPPER.**

25: **1**

26: **48, 64**. Alternately multiply by 3 and add previous
number i.e. 16 x 3 = 48 + 16 = 64
OR **192, 208**. Alternately multiply by previous number
and add previous number i.e. 16 x 12 = 192 + 16 = 208.

27: **SAME**

28: **a and c**

29: **10**. All columns add up to 30.

30: **BOO**

31: **SYDNEY**. All the others are capital cities.

32: **3**

33: **P, K**. Alternately add 3 and subtract 3
i.e. M + 3 = P and N - 3 = K.

34: **R**. Alternately add 2 and subtract 2
i.e. T - 2 = R.

35: **9**. Add the first column to the second column, then
divide by the third column i.e. (9 + 18) / 3 = 9.

36: **1097**. Multiply previous number by 3 and subtract 7,
for each number i.e. (368 x 3) - 7 = 1097.

37: **ALLIGATOR**

38: **P**. Add 2 to first column for second and add 4 to the
second column for the third i.e. L + 4 = P.

39: **TRUE**

40: **GGC**. Letters refer to position in alphabet
i.e. 429 + 344 = 773 = GGC.

Test 3 Answers

1: **7**. Opposites are halves.

2: **TNEUTMAOG**. Mangetout is a vegetable.
Cyan, Crimson and Sapphire are colours.

3: **PALM**

4: **6**

5: **18**. Add 3 to previous number.

6: **W**. Add 5 to previous letter.

7: **B = 36   F = 55   W = 21**

8: **EAT**

9: **DIFFERENT**

10: **30, 22**. Alternately subtract 8 and add 6.

11: **FALSE**. Some tennis rackets drink pencil sharpeners.

12: **K**. Words alternately spell TICK and TOCK.

13: **TRACT**

14: **PLUM**

15: **2**

16: **Z, H.** Top row add 5 and bottom subtract 5.

17: **N, L**. Alternately add 4 and subtract 2.

18: **96**. Add all outside numbers and multiply by 3.

19: **c and d**

20: **72, 54**. Alternately multiply by 4 and subtract previous number i.e. 18 x 4 = 72 - 18 = 54.

21: **EUCALYPTUS**

22: **1**

23: **YEARNING**

24: **SPA**

25: **90**. Multiply first row by second then double for third row i.e. 9 x 5 x 2 = 90.

26: **FALSE**. Some clocks make video recorders.

27: **P, R**. Alternately add 2 and subtract 2.

28: **CART**

29: **M**. Subtract 3 then subtract 6.

30: **21**. Multiply first row by second and add third.

31: **SYCAMORE**

32: **3**

33: **LION**. Only African animal.

34: **18**. Multiply bottom right number by 3.

35: **CANTEEN**

36: **88**. Double previous number then add 4.

37: **SAME**

38: **CAMP**. There is no 'C' in 'temporary'.

39: **TEKLESR**. Kestrel is a bird. Castanet, Lute and Glockenspiel, are musical instruments.

40: **S**. Alternately add 3 and subtract 3.

Test 4 Answers

1: **5**

2: **N**. Add 3 to previous letter.

3: **TRUE**

4: **C**. Word spells 'criminal' backwards.

5: **35**. Subtract 5 from previous number.

6: **PIN**

7: **7**. Subtract first row from second and divide by the third.

8: **POKER**

9: **226**. Add previous number +1, +2, etc.
i.e. 137 + 82 + 7 = 226.

10: **SING**

11: **15, 13**. Alternately subtract 2 and add 5.

12: **6**

13: **ORDER**

14: **O, N**. Alternately add 2 and subtract 1.

15: **96, 128**. Alternately multiply by 3 and add previous number.

16: **PURR** is a sound.
The others are animal parts.

17: **H**. Double position in alphabet along the row.

18: **BEZIQUE**

19: **SAME**

20: **10**. Divide number at the bottom by number on the right and subtract number on the left.

21: **ANINMOCN**. Cinnamon is a spice.
Jive, Fandango and Charleston are dances.

22: **L, O**. Alternately add 3 and subtract 2.

23: **2**

24: **CANASTA**

25: **END**

26: **FALSE**. Some sausages snore.

27: **82**. Subtract top number from bottom right.

28: **W = 29**   **G = 16**   **E = 40**

29: **b and c**

30: **4.** All rows add up to 54.

31: **5**

32: **CIVIL**

33: **890.** Add 3 and multiply by 2 each time.

34: **WASP**

35: **PATIENCE**

36: **SAME**

37: **R, E.** Top row add 1, 3, 5, 7 etc. and bottom subtract 2, 4, 6, 8 etc.

38: **KUPCNIHM.** Chipmunk is an animal. Elgar, Schubert and Stravinsky are composers.

39: **G.** Alternately add 4 and subtract 5.

40: **15**

Test 5 Answers

1:    **PEACH**. Peach is a fruit. The others are vegetables.

2:    **J = 48   K = 32   L = 18**

3:    **29**. Add 5 to previous number.

4:    **GRATING**

5:    **Q**. Add 4 to previous letter.

6:    **BOAT**

7:    **b and c**

8:    **MAZE**

9:    **3**

10:    **LIMB**

11:    **8, 12**. Alternately add 4 and subtract 2.

12:    **S, R**. Alternately add 3 and subtract 1.

13:    **TRUE**

14:    **81**. Subtract 4 from first column, add 5 to second and subtract 6 from third.

15: **STEAMER**

16: **5**. All rows add up to 34.

17: **DIFFERENT**

18: **BGANRYREOL**. Loganberry is a fruit. Lark, Penguin and Budgerigar are birds.

19: **36, 24**. Alternately multiply by 3 and subtract the previous number.

20: **3**

21: **120**. The bottom left number is 3 times the difference between the bottom right number and the top number, added to the top number.

22: **225**. Alternately multiply by 3 and subtract 15.

23: **ILL** and **EAT** are both valid answers.

24: **C**. Word spells 'contract' backwards.

25: **SEE**

26: **5**

27: **L, J**. Top row subtract 4, bottom add 3.

28: **S, K**. Alternately add 1 and subtract 3.

29: **TRUE**

30: **DIFFERENT**

31: **CRUISER**

32: **TINGE**. There is no 'I' in 'rectangle'.

33: **204**. Square 1, 2, 3 etc. and add previous number.

34: **BATTLESHIP**

35: **G**. Alternately add 5 and subtract 3.

36: **HEENVOBTE**. Beethoven is a composer.
Bean, Potato and Courgette are vegetables.

37: **HARRY**

38: **4**

39: **D**. Columns going right are half previous letter.

40: **64**. Double left number, add right number and
subtract bottom number for middle number.

Test 6 Answers

1: **12**. Subtract 6 from previous number.

2: **ATRIGU**. Guitar is a musical instrument.
Chair, Cupboard and Dresser are furniture.

3: **P**. Add 3 to previous letter.

4: **CIRCLE**

5: **40, 60**. Alternately add 20 and subtract 10.

6: **DIVE**

7: **3**

8: **R, Q**. Alternately add 2 and subtract 1.

9: **72**. Add left number to right number, multiply this by
bottom number to give middle number.

10: **THREAD**

11: **FALSE**. Some elephants can juggle six trees.

12: **TETRAHEDRON**

13: **897**. Multiply each number by 2 then subtract 1 to get
the next number i.e. (449 x 2) – 1 = 897.

14: **EXIT**

15: **R, G**. Alternately add 3 and subtract 1.

16: **1**

17: **TRAIL**. No 'T' in 'alarming'.

18: **K**. Two words alternately spell GOOD LUCK.

19: **TTMEODRRA**. Rotterdam is in Holland.
Brighton, Stratford and Manchester are in England.

20: **54, 81**. Alternately multiply by 2 and add
previous number.

21: **7**. All columns add up to 21.

22: **TRUE**

23: **FANCY**

24: **SAME**

25: **SOVEREIGN**. Sovereign is a gold coin.
Crown, Florin, Shilling and Sixpence are silver.

26: **P, D**. Top row add 2, bottom subtract 3.

27: **4**. Opposites are thirds.

28: **ART**

29: **4**

30: **29**. Add 7 to first column for second, then subtract 8 for third and then add 12 for fourth.

31: **1**

32: **21**. Subtract twice the difference between top and right from top for bottom left.

33: **T = 15   W = 38   Z = 40**

34: **SAME**

35: **RECTANGLE**

36: **U**. Opposites are triples.

37: **a and d**

38: **TEA**

39: **J**. Add 2 to each column.

40: **TRIANGLE**

1: **5**

2: **SLUTOC**. Locust is an insect. Plaice, Sardine and Mackerel are fish.

3: **39**. Add 8 to previous number.

4: **36**. Alternately add 8 and subtract 6.

5: **STALK**

6: **ICE**

7: **GREEN**

8: **7**. All rows add up to 45.

9: **18**. Each group of three numbers add up to 70.

10: **P**. Add 2 to previous letter.

11: **1**

12: **TRUE**

13: **K, I**. Add 2 to each letter to get the next-but-one letter along.

14: **DIFFERENT**

15: **MAGENTA**

16: **C**. Word spells 'campaign' backwards.

17: **ACT**

18: **11, 1**. Alternately subtract 10 and add 3.

19: **WAGNER**. Wagner is German.
The other composers are Austrian.

20: **W = 18   X = 29   Y = 50**

21: **Y, A**. Top row add 3, 6, 9 etc. , bottom row
subtract 3, 6, 9 etc.

22: **4**

23: **36, 54**. Alternately multiply by 2 and add
previous number.

24: **I**. Alternately add 2 and subtract 3.

25: **LEA**

26: **b and d**

27: **TANGERINE**

28: **128**. First row double each column, second triple and
third quadruple.

29: **TIMER**. There is no 'R' in 'complicate'.

30: **URGE**

31: **5**

32: **SUGATU**. August is a month. Jupiter, Pluto and Saturn are planets.

33: **64**. Opposites are quadruples.

34: **57**. Multiply left number by square of right number and divide by bottom number.

35: **TURQUOISE**

36: **SAME**

37: **X**. Add 3 to top letter to get middle letter, then add 4 to middle letter to get bottom letter.

38: **LEDGE**

39: **Y, D**. Alternately add 1 and subtract 2.

40: **TRUE**

Test 8 Answers

1: **6**. Subtract 7 from previous number.

2: **INCHKEC**. Chicken is an animal.
Cognac, Tequila and Champagne are drinks.

3: **V**. Add 5 to previous letter.

4: **KNiFE**

5: **34, 27**. Alternately subtract 7 and add 4.

6: **RISK**

7: **1**

8: **I, T**. Top row add 1, subtract 2, add 3 etc.
Bottom row subtract 1, add 2, subtract 3 etc.
i.e. M - 4 = I and P + 4 = T.

9: **OUT**

10: **TUMBLER**

11: **FALSE**. Cups never write poems.

12: **13**. Opposites add up to 19.

13: **BAR**

14: **36, 27**. Alternately multiply by 4 and subtract previous number.

15: **SAME**

16: **31**. All columns add up to 36.

17: **Q, O**. Alternately add 1 and subtract 2.

18: **5**

19: **98**. Multiply numbers in first column by 5, the second by 6, the third by 7 and the fourth by 8 i.e. 14 x 7 = 98.

20: **H, W**. Alternately add 2 and subtract 1.

21: **a and b**

22: **TWEEZERS**

23: **FALSE**. Muffins never watch television.

24: **1**

25: **4**. All numbers add up to 52.

26: **118**. Alternately multiply by 2 and add 5.

27: **BRENIMASU**. Submarine is a ship. Golf, Cricket and Squash are sports.

28: **P**. Two words alternately spell FULL STOP.

29: **SCREWDRIVER**

30: **VEST**

31: **K = 47**   **L = 18**   **M = 31**

32: **VOICE**. There is no 'C' in 'deviation'.

33: **HACKSAW**

34: **DEGRADE** and **DEFILE** are both valid answers.

35: **6**

36: **D**. Subtract 3 from top row and 2 from second.

37: **19**. Subtract the right number from the left number and divide by the bottom number.

38: **DIFFERENT**

39: **JUNE**. June has 30 days the others have 31.

40: **T**. Opposites are quadruples.

Converting Scores to IQs

The first stage is to work out your score for each of the eight tests. Give yourself one point for each item correctly solved; your score can range from 0 (none correct) to 40 (all correct). Then consult the conversion table, which will tell you which IQ rating corresponds to each score.

You will see that the conversion table shows scores in multiples of three, and IQ ratings in multiples of five. If your score falls between two of the scores shown, you can easily work out to which IQ rating it approximately corresponds. Greater accuracy would be a sham; your true IQ is likely to be within 5 points above or below the one you actually get from a single, self-administered half-hour test.

For a more accurate IQ rating, work out the average mark of all eight scores. Bear in mind, however, that as you are likely to get better as you learn how to do tests of this kind, the later tests are almost certain to give you a higher score than the first or second tests. You will gain between five and ten points of IQ through the 'test sophistication' you have acquired.

Technical Note

The tests were validated against the D.N. Jackson Multi-dimensional Aptitude Battery, using both the Verbal and Performance Scales. Test reliabilities are between .8 and .9.

Conversion Table

Score	IQ
3	90
6	95
9	100
12	105
15	110
18	115
21	120
24	125
27	130
30	135
33	140
36	145
39	150

FOR THE BEST IN PAPERBACKS, LOOK FOR THE

In every corner of the world, on every subject under the sun, Penguin represents quality and variety—the very best in publishing today.

For complete information about books available from Penguin—including Penguin Classics, Penguin Compass, and Puffins—and how to order them, write to us at the appropriate address below. Please note that for copyright reasons the selection of books varies from country to country.

In the United States: Please write to *Penguin Group (USA), P.O. Box 12289 Dept. B, Newark, New Jersey 07101-5289* or call 1-800-788-6262.

In the United Kingdom: Please write to *Dept. EP, Penguin Books Ltd, Bath Road, Harmondsworth, West Drayton, Middlesex UB7 0DA*.

In Canada: Please write to *Penguin Books Canada Ltd, 10 Alcorn Avenue, Suite 300, Toronto, Ontario M4V 3B2*.

In Australia: Please write to *Penguin Books Australia Ltd, P.O. Box 257, Ringwood, Victoria 3134*.

In New Zealand: Please write to *Penguin Books (NZ) Ltd, Private Bag 102902, North Shore Mail Centre, Auckland 10*.

In India: Please write to *Penguin Books India Pvt Ltd, 11 Panchsheel Shopping Centre, Panchsheel Park, New Delhi 110 017*.

In the Netherlands: Please write to *Penguin Books Netherlands bv, Postbus 3507, NL-1001 AH Amsterdam*.

In Germany: Please write to *Penguin Books Deutschland GmbH, Metzlerstrasse 26, 60594 Frankfurt am Main*.

In Spain: Please write to *Penguin Books S. A., Bravo Murillo 19, 1° B, 28015 Madrid*.

In Italy: Please write to *Penguin Italia s.r.l., Via Benedetto Croce 2, 20094 Corsico, Milano*.

In France: Please write to *Penguin France, Le Carré Wilson, 62 rue Benjamin Baillaud, 31500 Toulouse*.

In Japan: Please write to *Penguin Books Japan Ltd, Kaneko Building, 2-3-25 Koraku, Bunkyo-Ku, Tokyo 112*.

In South Africa: Please write to *Penguin Books South Africa (Pty) Ltd, Private Bag X14, Parkview, 2122 Johannesburg*.